Praise for *Food and Whine* by J

"A terrific book. . . . You could think of it . . . . , as a guide to cooking when you really feel like crying. . . . Enormously wise about the importance of food and family. . . . A warm, entertaining tale."

—Irene Sax, *Epicurious*

"For the mom who prefers to laugh at her oft-challenging lot in life."

—Patti Thorn, *Rocky Mountain News*

"Funny, incisive . . . will hit home with moms who are busy juggling career, kids, and cooking."

—*Bon Appetit*

"A wonderful memoir cum cookbook that is alive with humor and compassion. . . . Delightful. . . . Its easy manner belies the intelligent observation of a harried mother who has an original, sensible outlook on the chaotic world in which we live."

—Laura Philpot Benedict, *The Grand Rapids Press*

"Funny stuff about the unfunny business of being a mom and wife in the '90s."

—Greg Langley, *The Advocate* (Baton Rouge, LA)

"Funny and poignant. . . . Entertaining . . . like Erma Bombeck on acid."

—Susan Shapiro, *The Jerusalem Report*

"Laugh-out-loud funny, ironic, frank, fearful, neurotic, warm, and engaging . . . witty, moving."

—*Kirkus Reviews*

"A great first book by essayist Moses, who has been touted as the Erma Bombeck of the boomer generation."

—*Library Journal*

"A laugh-out-loud, book-length monologue. It has the daring, free association of stand-up comedy, as well as the comic's sad kernel of truth at the center of each observation."

—*Jewish Family and Life*

"If David Letterman were to write a cookbook, it might read something like this. Moses' lively anecdotes about family life are interspersed with tongue-in-cheek recipes that . . . will provide solace to the most harried."

—*Moment* magazine

"*Food and Whine* is more than funny: while Jennifer Moses fills us with Banana Bombs, Duck à l'Orange à la Mom, and Mediterranean-Roasted New Potatoes 'that even her husband can make,' she also gives us a tender vision of family joy and chaos. Her recipes are instructions for loving. In the midst of her busy life, this mother pauses to reveal the most delicate moments of grace between children and parents, brothers and sisters, husbands and wives. Jennifer Moses offers her readers a glimpse of how they might face their own deepest fears and sorrows."

—Melanie Rae Thon, author of *Iona Moon* and *First, Body*

"This book has a limited audience. The only people who will find it funny will be women and men. Women will like it for the caustic yet touching exploration of the complex, multilayered relationship between the genders. Men will like it for the sex."

—Gene Weingarten, author of *The Hypochondriac's Guide to Life and Death*

"Jennifer Moses writes with wit and verve about the fearful clatter of children, harried domesticity, and clanging pots. When the kid-stained chintz curtain parts, we see a serious writer at work, and then the constant whine becomes a timeless lament."

—Andrei Codrescu, NPR commentator and author of *Messiah*

Food AND Whine

Confessions of a
New Millennium Mom

JENNIFER MOSES

A FIRESIDE BOOK
PUBLISHED BY SIMON & SCHUSTER
NEW YORK LONDON TORONTO SYDNEY SINGAPORE

FIRESIDE
Rockefeller Center
1230 Avenue of the Americas
New York, NY 10020

First Fireside Edition 2000
FIRESIDE and colophon are registered trademarks of
Simon & Schuster, Inc.

Designed by Ruth Lee

Manufactured in the United States of America

1   3   5   7   9   10   8   6   4   2

The Library of Congress has cataloged the
Simon & Schuster edition as follows:
Moses, Jennifer.
Food and whine: confessions of an end of the
millennium mom/ Jennifer Moses.
p.   cm.
1. Housewives—Humor   2. Motherhood—Humor.
3. Women—Humor.   I. Title.
PN6231.H74M67 1999
814'.54—dc21   98-51154   CIP
ISBN 0-684-84837-6
0-684-86562-9 (Pbk)
Parts of *Food and Whine* have appeared in
slightly different form in *The Washington Post,*
Inside, Bon Appetit, and *Working Mother.*

CONTENTS

For my mother

Buns in the Oven

 I NEVER CONSCIOUSLY PLANNED to become a mother, although I shouldn't really have been so surprised when, after weeks and weeks of both not using birth control *and* having sex, I discovered that I was pregnant. I knew this because when I went to my doctor to pee in a plastic cup, he said: "You're pregnant." My response was to plunge into an anxiety attack.

It wasn't that I didn't want children per se. I was a married woman with a steady job and a nice husband, and on the brink of thirty. Nevertheless, I wasn't *ready*. There were a lot of things that I had yet to accomplish. For example, I was not yet a movie star. Nor had my first novel been published to great acclaim, finally proving to my enormous and incredibly competitive extended family that I am not, after all, a person whose greatest intellectual talent had to do with putting color-coordinated outfits on. The hitch was that I hadn't yet written a novel. I didn't so much as have an idea for a novel. I was so upset by the news of my impending motherhood that I couldn't summon the concentration to *read* a novel. I hadn't, in fact, distinguished myself in any way, unless you count the time, when I was a freshman in college, that I stood on a table in the middle of the university theater stage and screamed about the bugs that were crawling all over my skin, in a Sam Shepard one-act called *Red Cross*. Not to mention that despite having spent years in psychotherapy, I was still having that same odd dream about having group sex with a bunch of Hasidic Jews in New York's Union Square while my mother—a Bloomingdales shopping bag in hand—looked on.

In other words, my most pressing fantasies for myself never included children, who, as most people know, demand a lot of attention and spit up a lot. *Yes, yes*, I'd tell my husband, *children, uh-huh, whatever.* Then I'd think about the big, charming Victorian house with the hardwood floors and enormous windows and antique furniture and Oriental rugs where I'd live with my children, *after* I became a famous writer and showed my brilliant cousins, who all went to Harvard or Yale, that although I flunked trigonometry and barely made it through high school Spanish, I am in fact a literary genius.

Har-har, joke's on me, because here I am, ten years later, dangerously close to forty and the mother of three, and I still haven't received a National Book Award. Nor do I hang around with writers and artists all day long, sipping chardonnay and talking about Proust. Nor is my house filled with early American antiques and hand-loomed Oriental rugs, but rather, with Power Ranger paraphernalia and a lot of other cheap plastic toys designed to offend my deepest sensibilities. Even so, I really REALLY love my kids. I like them, too—so much that I have decided, after all, to believe in God.

In a nutshell: First, the first kid got born. Then, some three years later, I became pregnant with twins. And being pregnant with twins isn't fun at all. This is what happens when you're pregnant with twins: Not only do you swell up to the size of a small hippopotamus, prompting total strangers to point and say rude things such as, "My God you're huge," but you throw up all the time. I had round-the-clock morning sickness. Can you say: Please pass the Saltines? The nausea eventually passed, but I became so big that toward the end of my pregnancy, I had to get out of bed in order to turn over in bed, and people kept patting my stomach and saying: "Instant family." No. *Wrong.* There is absolutely *nothing* instant about carrying two small people for nine months, and then actually giving birth to them, a process that might have been more enjoyable if I hadn't personally had to be there.

But now we have Sam, Rose, and Jonathan, and if I do say so myself, they are magnificent children. Even the boys, who, being boys, will no doubt grow up to be men, a concept that I have some trouble with. I don't really trust men. For one thing, they're so proud of their doinkers that they have *names* for them: Mr. P., or Superman, or Stud Hero Guy. My boys are already so fascinated with their little ding-dongs that it really makes me wonder. And I don't *really* mind the Kellogg's Just Right cereal smeared onto the kitchen wall, or the snot that permanently dried into the upholstery of our vaguely Victorian "Tuscan Gold" living room sofa, or the fact that my breasts, once so—shall we say bright and bouncy?—are now candidates for emergency plastic surgery. My husband used to look better too. At least my hair's not falling out. But if it were, do you think *he'd* dust-bust it away every morning? Or Windex the little tooth droppings that fly onto the bathroom mirror when you floss? Can the man even run a vacuum cleaner? Does he know where in the house we so much as keep it? In other words, did I, after all those years of psychotherapy—culminating with my most recent attempt, with a woman who turned out to be a friend of my across-the-street neighbor and whose kid I actually almost ran over once (which would make for great psychoanalytic material if it hadn't actually happened)—go ahead and marry my father after all?

The thing about my father is: you really wouldn't

want to marry him. True, he's cute—but he's also constitutionally incapable of doing laundry, washing dishes, or cleaning up fresh spit-up. It's a fifties thing, I guess. Of course, my mother married him. And I distinctly remember wanting to marry him too. I was three, four years old. I was so small, standing there, looking up, proposing marriage. "But what would we do with Mommy?" he said. "Throw her out?" Those were his exact words. I know this because I spent four years and tens of thousands of dollars in psychoanalysis, and this is the kind of material that shrinks live for. "Heads up!" shrinks say when they see me coming. "We've got a live one." Psychotherapy is, in fact, the one thing I've been able really to excel at, but it isn't the kind of thing I can put on my resumé (*1982–1992: Psychotherapeutic Patient: Duties included free association, crying jags, psychosomatic stomachaches, transference, resistance, irrational fears, insomnia, and self-pity*). But if it *were* the kind of thing you could put on a resumé, I'd have it all over my older sister, Binky, who went to Harvard Law School and now lives in this totally gorgeous apartment with a view of Central Park—not that I'm still caught up in any kind of sibling rivalry just because our father preferred her. Not to mention that it would give me something to say at cocktail parties when people ask: "What do you *do?*" After all, you can't just say: "I have three kids, so mainly I change diapers and wipe snot." No one, in my experience, wants to hear this.

As I was saying, the motherhood thing sort of crept up on me, until one day, not long ago, I found myself wandering the back-to-school aisles of our local Wal-Mart, lost in a fantasy that had me cruising the malls in a brand-new minivan. Which isn't the kind of fantasy I used to have at all. I *used* to fantasize about being asked out by Richard Gere. Actually, that's not quite accurate either. I used to fantasize about being asked out by Woody Allen, who—spotting me across a crowded book store one day—would recognize a kindred spirit, take me to lunch, invite me to write his next movie, and then hit on me.

At any rate, one day not long afterward, I looked up from the refrigerator, where I'd been searching for something "fresh" in my "fresh vegetable" drawer, and I realized that I was having a nervous breakdown. Because once again, my kids were screaming and beating on each other, I spent too much of my life in Wal-Mart, the sink was backed up, and I had to make dinner. And I don't even like to cook. Meanwhile my husband was just sitting there, reading the newspaper.

"Fuck," I said.

"Jesus, Jen," my husband said. "Not in front of the kids."

"What does *fuck* mean, Mommy?" Sam, our eldest, said.

Then my husband and I got into this really dumb fight about why he gets to go to the office and wear nice clothes while I have to stay home and get wee-

weed on, and he said: "If you're so frustrated why don't you stop kvetching and *do* something?" Then he pointed out—and this is what REALLY got me mad—that he'd always encouraged me to find meaningful work, even if that meant his rearranging his schedule so he could shoulder more of the child care.

"When is my penis going to be as big as yours, Daddy?" Sam asked.

Right then and there I decided to write a book. No more short stories and beginnings of novels for me! *This* book was going to be about me and kids and food—not gourmet cuisine of the Julia Child school but the really delicious slapping-it-together stuff that my mother had taught me to make. It wouldn't give much in the way of hard information such as yield, exact measurement, and pan size, though—because when *I* cook, it's all I can do to locate the refrigerator. And as far as I can tell, most mothers of small children cook the same way: in a full, outright panic, grabbing whatever isn't speckled with mold, throwing it in a pot, and calling it "dinner."

All I needed was a title. How about *K'vitchen K'vetch?* I thought. Or *In the Kitchen with Mosey?* Oprah's chef made a bundle on it. Why not me? Even better: *In the K'vitchen K'vetching with Mosey.* It would be about family and food and love and mess, about feeding my kids and fending off ontological anxiety. And it would have *recipes*—and not the usual sort either, with their simplistic do-this-and-then-do-that format for homemade whole wheat pappardelle with chicken-liver-and-olive sauce—but, rather, the recipes that my sisters and most of the other women in my family (and me too) use, the kind that any idiot can tackle with fairly delicious results and that, as a bonus, happen to be the ones I know.

The more I thought about my book, the more it occurred to me that although I once lived in New York and spent the better part of my "leisure time" either waiting for some guy who didn't even know I was alive to call me—either that or trying to figure out how to tactfully disengage my upper parts from the paws of some bozo or another whose last name I wasn't completely sure of—I now have no leisure time. Instead, I have breakfast time, snack time, lunch time, snack time, dinner time, bath time, and after-dinner-snack time. In other words, I spend the greater part of my waking hours feeding people. And I still don't have the slightest idea how to get around in my own damn kitchen! Even so, I've got a million recipes floating around in my head. How about *Mamma Makes Leftovers* or *Mamma's Movable Feast?*

As my kids, growing frantic, complained that they were starving to death, my project grew. For whereas once I cooked maybe twice a year—usually a romantic dinner consumed on the rooftop of the East Village walk-up I lived in when I was single and that my mother was afraid of visiting because, as she pointed out, there were drug dealers across the street—I now coveted a Williams Sonoma rice cooker. How had it happened? One minute I was, let's face facts, this way-cool hip chick who wore nothing but black and drank cappuccino with burgeoning performance artists with pierced body parts—and the next minute I was Mrs. Mom. How about *Cooking the Frantic Way* or *Out of the Frying Pan, into the Fire?* Mere moments after my book's publication, Oprah personally would call me to invite me onto her show. At which point I'd have a chance to tell her about how ironic it is that, despite my limited culinary skills, all kinds of people, including my mother-in-law, like my cooking. I envisioned myself explaining to Oprah about how the book had evolved from a single brilliant title—how about *Whining and Dining?*—to a year-in-the-life-of romp through my kitchen. How about *Everything But the Kitchen Sink Cuisine?* Or *Chefs Like It Hot?*

And when, later, I ran these titles by my husband, he said: "Why don't you stop fantasizing about going on *Oprah* and sit down and write the damn thing?"

I was about to protest that that was easy for *him* to say—after all, he actually got things done when he put his mind to it—when I opened the freezer and saw, mercifully, that there was a full container of chocolate-chip cookie-dough ice cream in it.

"There is a God," I said.

And a moment later, as if drawn to the kitchen by some sixth sense all of their own, the kids were crowding around, begging for their after-dinner snacks.

ONE

They Only Take Tips

LET ME BEGIN AT THE BEGINNING, or at least at the beginning of my adventures in motherhood, which began for me with my first child, Sam. The birth of a Jewish boy is such a joyous occasion that the first thing the mother of such a child is expected to do is plan a party for him. The event is called a *bris,* and it celebrates the infant's getting his little wanker snipped in accordance with Jewish law.

That being said, during the entire time I was pregnant with Sam, I had very mixed feelings about the entire deal—not just the *bris,* but the whole concept of reproduction. Perhaps the problem was that we were then living in Los Angeles, and people assumed that because I (a) had a long, dark braid down my back and

(b) was pregnant, I was also Mexican, and could answer such questions as: "¿Crée que George Bush se comporta asi porqué tiene un peñe pequenito?" This was very confusing.

I kept dreaming that I'd given birth to a chicken. My mother-in-law called every other day from her home in Philadelphia to tell me that once the baby "popped out," the discomfort would all be worth it—and, by the way, had I thought about signing up for classes on how to decorate an infant's room, like her friend Edna's niece Cathy who lived in Melrose Park and was married to a neurologist? On the days when my mother-in-law didn't call, my mother, just outside Washington, D.C., did. She told me that, for her, giving birth had been "a snap." It had? My mother had had four cesarean sections, and her stomach was ribbed and mottled and scarred, as if covered with melted rubber bands. Toward the end of my pregnancy, Mom called twice daily. Here's what she said: "Anything new?" Then my mother-in-law, who sometimes mixes her metaphors, would call and say, "A watched pot never rises, but don't worry because yours will." And I'd sit around our small, dingy apartment and worry about my ability simply to *get the baby out,* even if it was a chicken.

Fortunately, I was still in therapy, so I knew that my anxieties were irrational, except that they weren't, because how the hell was it possible that I could give birth to anything, let alone a child, thus rendering me someone's *mother?* But when I finally went into labor, it wasn't a chicken, but Sam, who emerged, all covered with slime and looking just like E.T. The whole room seemed to glow, as if with holy light.

I was flooded with love, transported, as if kissed by angels. Nothing prepared me for the feeling of sheer transcendence that I experienced the first few hours after Sam's birth. I had, after all, created a masterpiece. (I still contend that babies are almost entirely the creations of their mothers.) He was so beautiful. He was so perfect. His skin felt like mist. His breath smelled like cookies. I went around in this cloud of happiness for two, maybe three days, until, at last, sleep deprivation caught up with me, and I seriously began to consider the ramifications of what I had done.

Giving birth to the twins was a different kind of experience, even though at least one of the books I read on the subject assured me that if I kept to a macrobiotic diet and never *ever* ate an entire quart of Ben and Jerry's chocolate-chip cookie-dough ice cream at one sitting again, I would have such a healthy pregnancy that, if I chose to, I could deliver my twins in the privacy of my own home, attended only by my male or female partner, and my midwife. God, I hated those books. Midwife? Frankly, I'm more a male-dominated-medical-establishment kind of gal. By this time, we had long since left Los Angeles. Now we were living in Washington, D.C., where everyone is either an associate at a giant law firm specializing in suing people or a partner in a giant law firm specializing in suing people. In fact, my husband had become one of those associates at a giant downtown law firm, meaning that it was astonishing that he was home long enough to make a baby to begin with. And this time he'd helped make not one, but *two*. And right afterward, he'd nuzzled me, stretched, and logged onto Lexis/Nexis to do a little legal research. Not really, of course. Even so, one way or another, this was not going to be one of your poetic, low-fat, crystal-enhanced, Southern California births. Thus, when the time came—long after my neighbors had grown bored taking bets about whether I'd deliver my babies by simply bursting open at the seams one day as I waddled down the sidewalk—I was wheeled straight into the delivery room, which was decorated in various soothing shades of stainless steel, and hydraulically lifted onto a birthing platform. Where, just as the books had described, I had an intimate birthing experience: It was just me, my husband, my doctor, my labor nurse, the anesthesiologist, two emergency neonatologists, four obstetric residents, two pediatricians, two pediatric nurses, a few stray first-year residents who happened to be hanging around that day, and several attorneys. Just kidding about the attorneys! In truth, the only attorney in the room was my husband. He was holding my hand and whispering something about the brief that he had to have finished by the next day, and would I mind very much if, after I had finished my own little project, he went to the office for a few hours? Just kidding again! Actually, I don't remember what he was saying because his words were drowned out by the sound of some shrewish, hysterical woman screaming, "Get them out! Get them out!"

"Ready?" my doctor said at last. Ready? I'd been ready for at least four months. "When is it going to be over?" I asked. "That's the spirit, Jen," he said. And he took out his vacuum and vacuum-suctioned first my daughter, and then my son, out into the world.

Rose and Jonathan.

The nurse placed them in my arms.

Okay, I thought. Thank God, they're healthy. More to the point, thank God they're OUT. But NOW WHAT? It's one thing to bring home one single teeny-tiny baby, as we'd done four years earlier with Sam, especially because my mother had flown out to L.A. to help us take care of him. Actually my mother-in-law came too. That was interesting. One baby, two first-time Jewish grandmothers. It's a miracle that no one was hurt. But the point is that when Sam was born, there were four adults and one baby. The ratio wasn't perfect, but it was manageable. But this time there were two of them, and only two of us, and—this is where things got really tricky—we also had Sam. Remember him? Your first-born? The little boy who would soon be regressing, wetting his bed, throwing five-alarm fits over nothing, and being visited by imaginary bees? We didn't want him to get lost in the shuffle, just because he was no longer tiny and sweet and adoring and perfect, but loud and hyper and demanding, not to mention permanently coated with a thin layer of spaghetti sauce, and come to think of it, maybe he *was* ready for boarding school. *Uh-oh,* I thought.

I didn't know how I was going to manage. And it wasn't as if I had the option of sending one of them back, with a little note, like the ones I routinely sent to Eddie Bauer, indicating that even though the dress I'd ordered looked great on the model in the catalogue, it made me look like a watermelon.

"I love you, Jen," my husband said as I was lying there with my two sticky newborns in either arm. He looked as if he meant it too.

Yeah, right, I thought.

Which brings me to my next point. To this day, people often ask me how I "got" twins. What they really want to know is whether I used fertility drugs, and if so, which kinds. So I want to take the opportunity to clear the record right now, even though what I'm about to say is somewhat embarrassing, and it might result in my having a lot of uncomfortable and strained visits with my father, because even though he paid for my wedding and thus knows I got married, and knows, also, that in August of 1989 I gave birth to his first grandchild, what he—being a Jewish father—doesn't know is the following: My husband and I had sex.

It was (I remember it precisely) the night after my husband's law firm's annual Christmas extravaganza,

and because this time I was desperately trying to
get pregnant, I knew that I was, er, ripe. My husband and I got all dressed up and went downtown, where we stood around eating spring rolls with
a bunch of people who all began every conversation
with some mention of billable hours—except for the
partners, who all began every conversation with some
mention of their vacation homes in Martha's Vineyard.
Afterward, even though we were stuffed, we went out
to a restaurant with some of my husband's lawyer
friends from the firm. The idea was that the more intimate setting would enhance the conversation about
billable hours and how hard it is to make partner these
days. And some time during this party, I started yawn-
ing and making remarks about how much I missed being around the kind of interesting people I used to
hang out with in New York before I got married—people who were able to sustain a conversation about
something other than, say, the use of corporate torts
in the deregulation of the cable television industry.
For some reason, my observations pissed my husband
off, and he and I ended up getting into a fight. We
fought all the way from the restaurant to the car, and
all the way up Rock Creek Parkway to our house, and
all the way up the stairs, where we went to separate
bathrooms to brush our teeth and put our jammers
on, and from there to our respective sides of the bed,
where I said, "Figure out some way or another to plant
the seed," and he said, "Let's just get this wretched

experience over with." And *that's* how we got twins.

And I knew right away that I was pregnant, because within days of our tender lovefest I started throwing up, and then, after I learned that I was pregnant with twins, my anxiety level, which, on a scale of one to ten, is usually hovering around nine, shot all the way up to *twelve!* I started calling my shrink and crying into the phone, begging her to put me on Prozac, or Valium, or Nyquil—*anything* to please take the anxiety away. And you know what she said? She said: "Well, it certainly sounds as if you have a lot to talk about." Which is all they *ever* say! Just once I'd like my psychiatrist to turn to me and say: "I'm putting you on intravenous Prozac right this very minute." But when at last I was sitting face to face with her, looking at my feet and sobbing about being taken over by babies, she didn't breathe a word about medicating me. Instead, she said, "Well, it certainly sounds as if you have some issues gestating." And she wasn't even making a pun! That's when it dawned on me that my psychiatrist couldn't even *begin* to understand what I was going through. How could she? After all, was she forced to tell people at cocktail parties that she stayed home wiping up baby spit when they asked *her* what she "did"? I think not. I think, rather, that when people at cocktail parties asked her, "But what do *you* do?" she answered, "In addition to my role of mother, in which I both nurture and set boundaries, I'm also a psychoanalytically trained psychiatrist specializing in treating self-pitying housewives whose grandiose fantasies typically contain a fair admixture of hostile paranoia."

My husband, too, was slightly flipped out about the prospect of having twins, and went around telling jokes about my new-found resemblance to the late Allan Sherman. And I was still only in my second month.

The one person who was truly thrilled about my being pregnant with twins was my mother-in-law, Lola. Her husband (my husband's father, Stanley) had died of cancer in 1985, and though she was lonely, and often plain sad, she'd thrown herself into the role of grandmother with tremendous enthusiasm. As far as Grandma Lola was concerned, the more babies, the better. One night when she called to see how I was feeling and I told her that I was just too nauseated to be happy about having twins, she said: "I know, Jennifer, but you can't make babies without breaking eggs." At which point she started making soup and freezing it, and she didn't stop until seven months later, when my twins were born.

As I was saying, I ended up giving birth to Rose and Jonathan on August 14, a Saturday. On Monday we were kicked out of the hospital and sent home, to a place where there's no one to bring you food on a tray, or watch over your newborn twins day and night to make sure that their body temperatures are normal and that they don't somehow swallow their own tongues, or to help you to the toilet in the middle of the night when your legs are about to give out, owing to the fact that your body is still kind of beat up from pushing two, count them, TWO, babies out of your private place.

It didn't help that Sam came home from nursery school that day with a fever of 103 degrees. He was a hot little red-faced muffin. He had all this green gook dripping out of his nose. He came up the stairs to see me—after all, I'm his *mother*—threw up on me, then rubbed his little vomit-covered face on my shoulder. The twins, who had been sleeping on our bed, woke up and began to wail. My husband stood around saying: "Oh my God. Oh my God." Fortunately I was an experienced mother by this point, and knew what to do. The thing to do when you've just brought two-day-old twins home from the hospital and your four-year-old comes home from school with a contagious disease is this: Burst into tears.

It was all a little overwhelming, and I still wasn't sure I really liked my new kids all that much. Jonathan was kind of on the scrawny side: He looked like a bird. My mother kept saying, "He doesn't look like *our* side of the family at all." Rose was, at the very least, more noticeably human—her skin was pink and her face was round—but already she had developed the annoying habit of waking up the very instant that her twin brother had fallen back to sleep. Also, neither one was a very good conversationalist. On the other hand, they did cry a lot.

This is how the twin thing works: It's 12:59 A.M., time for bed. Not that you can sleep. You're too tired to sleep. Instead, you're lying in bed, the theme song from "Barney" going round and round your brain, and wondering why every time your mother-in-law makes a sandwich, she leaves all your cutlery drawers open, such that all the crumbs and bologna tails drop in and co-mingle with your knives and forks. Come to think of it, your husband does the same thing. Perhaps it's genetic. Perhaps you've spawned the next generation of crumb-and-lettuce-bits droppers. Will you ever sleep again? If not, would it be considered "good-enough parenting" to put Jonathan in the basement for a few hours, so you won't hear him crying? YOU DIDN'T MEAN THAT. You love your kids. You love them so much that already they are your whole life— the air you breathe, your blood and your bones. Go to sleep. Why bother? Any minute now, one of them is going to wake up, so there's really no point in falling asleep, even though your husband, whom you once— you're sure of it—adored, *is* sleeping, thereby proving that he is a jerk. You already knew he was a jerk anyway. Who else but a jerk could sleep at a time like this? If *you* fall asleep, how will you hear it when one of them stops breathing? Perhaps it's time to get up and check. Why did you get married?

Then one twin gets up, then the other gets up, then the first one spits up on you, and then, finally, after you've settled both babies down, and changed from your soiled nightgown into a slightly less soiled one, Sam gets up crying because he made wee-wee in his bed, plus a bunch of gorillas are hiding in his closet. Then all three of them somehow end up in your bed, jammed up between you and your husband.

What I'm trying to illustrate is this: I was in no shape to be present for, much less to plan, the first big event in a Jewish boy's life. Namely, the subject that I'm trying to get around to: the *bris*.

These days, a lot of people seem to take issue with the idea that God Himself demands that Jewish boys undergo ritual circumcision. People think it's barbaric, and weird, and tribal, and bizarre—that it has nothing to do with spiritual maturity, or covenant, or living by God's will. My own feeling is that circumcision is a good, good thing. I mean, if you don't snip it when they're tiny babies, you end up with this doinker that looks like a little old one-eyed man dressed in slimy gray rags. Plus I didn't spend all those happy carefree childhood hours in the woods that surrounded our house in Virginia playing "Let's Hide from the Nazis" for nothing. And *so.* I am Jewish, as are my children. We were going to have a *bris,* and while we were at it, we were going to have a naming ceremony for Rose, because I was damned if Jonathan was the only one who was going to be getting in good with the Big Guy. There was another reason, too, for our having decided to do a double ceremony. Namely: My mother and my mother-in-law were involved in a heated competition for the affections of our children, and this way, each grandmother could have a baby on her lap.

Let me elaborate on this point. The grandmothers, bless their hearts, did not as a rule annoy or upset each other. But they both found their children—i.e., *us*—to be somewhat troublesome. As far as they were concerned, we were a necessary evil, to be humored in the name of a greater cause.

Here's a dramatization of what I mean:

My mother ("dropping by" my house because she "just happened to be in the neighborhood" to give me a three-month-old copy of the *New Yorker* that she thinks I ought to read even though she knows I have my own subscription because she was the one who had given it to me last Hanukkah). (Speaking to Sam, now about three, in extremely cheerful voice). "What are you doing today? Are you having fun? Look what Grammy brought you!" (Produces a shiny red tricycle.)

My mother-in-law (driving up to our house two days later, her car laden with little plastic bags filled with doodads, and then getting out and hugging Sam, now about three). "What are you wearing?" (To me, in very loud voice): "My God, Jennifer, can't you get him some decent clothes?" (Returning to my son): "Guess what Grandma Lola brought you!" (Produces combination tape deck/CD player).

Gentiles are often puzzled by what goes on at a *bris*. They feel uncomfortable. They don't know where to look, what to say, how to act. Actually, most Jews, including the newborn's parents, don't know what to do either. There is, for example, the question of payment.

Q: Do you have to pay the *mohel* (a Jewish man, often a rabbi, who specializes in circumcision) for his services?

A: No, they only take tips.

Here's what we did: We called a rabbinical *mohel,* who patiently told us what to expect, and then we called the caterer, because the main thing about a *bris*/naming ceremony is this: After the little ones have been trimmed and named and introduced to your people and to God, everyone goes back to the dining room and chows down, while *you,* the mother, the one whose body now resembles an overstuffed Glad bag, goes upstairs and changes a few diapers. Yes, it's a party! For everyone, that is, but you. For you, it's a crisis. It's World War Three, right there in your living room.

And yet I had given birth to healthy twins, a feat I had not been at all certain I'd be able to perform. How many women did I know who were desperately trying to have children but couldn't? And I had *three.* Now all I needed to do, other than raise them, was figure out how to be their mother and somehow hold onto some remnant of myself.

A friend of mine, or maybe it was me, once said: "Motherhood isn't an identity, it's a job description." But so far, with Sam, I hadn't done a very good job at either the job description or the identity part. From the get-go, Sam had needed a lot of attention—and I mean *a lot*—and yet no matter how many games of "Mommy the Pony" we played, or how many versions of "three-hour-long shit fit" we experimented with, he still wanted more of me (more attention, more hugs, more games, more food), and was still anxious, clingy, and very very loud, leading me to conclude that, as a mother, I stunk. On the other hand, I was a failure as a career woman too—but only because, as a "stay-at-home" mom, I didn't have a career.

In my little corner of Washington, D.C., this was a big no-no. On my street alone, there were moms who doubled as doctors *and* as lawyers, and you can bet that not one of them moped around their houses dreaming up clever answers to the cocktail party question: "But what do you *do?*" How, indeed, could taking care of a single child be so draining?

Finally, when he was old enough—in his case, two—I'd put Sam in two-day-a-week nursery school. The idea was that this arrangement would give me a little time to write short stories that would never get published. Of course, this setup didn't exactly solve my problems. For one thing, I felt extremely guilty about putting him in school at such a tender age, or, as my mother put it: "You're putting Sam in *day care?*" She had a point: My selfish action practically guaranteed that Sam would grow up to be a sociopath or, perhaps, a heroin addict. While Sam was in nursery school, I sat in front of my computer, worrying about what all those perky, sweet, young teachers were *doing* to him, and getting an ulcer. I tried to make it up to him in the afternoons by pushing him on the swing until my arms ached and I was so bored that I felt as if I was going to explode. Meanwhile, all my efforts to launch my literary career had produced nothing but rejection slips and the promise of complete and annihilating obscurity.

Now it was two years later. We had two more children—two lovely, healthy, living, breathing human creatures—and we were introducing them to God. All the relatives were gathered in our living room. But already, as the rabbi intoned the beautiful Hebrew prayers, and the sun slanted in through our living room windows, I heard the small, distinct voice of David Letterman saying: Have you ever considered moving to Tahiti?

It seems as if the whole day happened in a dream. Yet there, in our photograph album, are my mother and my mother-in-law, sitting side by side on our living room sofa, a baby in each lap. They look happy. My mother is wearing a pretty silk dress, and she looks younger—far younger—than she is. She is, in fact, enjoying her last weeks of health and serenity—but we didn't know it then. My father, silver haired, is hunkered down in the corner, shmoozing with the rabbi. My husband and I look washed out, exhausted, but somehow contented. Sam and his cousin, having fought and made up, swagger, their arms wrapped over one another's shoulders, indifferent to everything but one another. And there are other people too: my grandmother, who was about to turn ninety; my husband's brother and sister; my brother and his family; and my father's old friend, Milton, who still, in his seventies, rode his bicycle to work.

Yes, the *bris* served a purpose. I mean, other than getting on good terms with the Big Guy. It showed me that I'm capable of having a nervous breakdown while simultaneously eating three bagels slathered with cream cheese and lox.

It also provided us with leftovers. And then the food ran out. So I called my mother. If memory serves, I was awake: Therefore I was in hysterics. Sobbing, I told her that I wasn't at all sure that I properly loved my children, and I wasn't at all sure that I even *liked* my husband, and I was so fat and flabby that I'd never ever wear anything other than sweatpants and my husband's old college sweatshirt again until I died and was buried in a shroud. I told her that as a result of my selfishness, I had already ruined Sam's life. I also told her that I couldn't see being the kind of old-fashioned prefeminist mother that she herself was—by which I meant being a mother who selflessly served her children's needs while ignoring her own—and then I begged her to come over to my house that very minute to take care of me. And do you know what she said? She said that she couldn't, because—*get this*—she wasn't feeling well. "I kind of feel like maybe I have a bomb in my side," she said.

Excuse me? A bomb in her side? A little old psychosomatic ouch? Selfish witch. You see, my mother simply doesn't get sick. Because if she did, who'd take care of everybody? I was about to tell her that a cup of tea might make the "bomb" disappear, when she said something even more annoying: She told me that soon I'd be coping just fine. "The first thing you have to do," she said, in the perky, matter-of-fact voice that she uses when she wants to let me know that she is actually Wilma Flintstone, "is to get out of your nightgown and into the kitchen."

Did she say *into the kitchen?* Who did she think I was? Her?

"But I don't really like to cook," I said.

"I know," she said. "I didn't really like to cook either."

This was news to me. After all, my mother had spent the past thirty or forty years in the kitchen. *And* she was a good cook.

I was, in a word, horrified. But of course, like Wilma Flintstone, she was right. Because not only is eating better than not eating, but also, seeing that (a) I could barely remember my premarriage life of nonstop glamour at various New York hot spots, and (b) my literary career was in East Nowheresville, I figured I may as well learn to make kugel.

Mom also taught me another lesson about motherhood. To wit: You're going to spend a lot of time in the kitchen, so you may as well like the wallpaper. Which is why I eventually stripped mine— this really tacky yellow and green stuff covered with pictures of fruits—and replaced it with a faux-speckled blue sponge-paint job.

The other thing, of course, is this: The nicest present anyone can possibly give new parents is food, the cooked kind, like the marvelous cabbage soup that my mother-in-law made for us, and froze, when my twins were little more than tadpoles. I've recorded it, and all the other recipes that I've been given and that I use, in the hopes of demonstrating the following proposition: If I can cook, anyone can.

I'd always been intimidated by soup, but this recipe, I've learned, is user friendly. The trick is to remember to go out with a shopping list and buy all the ingredients *ahead* of time. That way you won't give up before you start, and end up ordering soggy, overpriced carryout.

Here is Grandma Lola's cabbage soup that she learned from Aunt Shirley. It yields about six servings.

2 tablespoons vegetable oil
2 pounds short ribs of beef trimmed of fat (or use a
    chunk of meat like brisket or pot roast)
2 chopped onions
2 cups sliced carrots
Minced garlic

1½ quarts water

1 big can crushed tomatoes

1 sliced head green cabbage

Salt and pepper to taste

1 bay leaf

¼ cup lemon juice

¼ cup packed brown sugar

Handful gingersnaps, smashed

In large pot, heat oil over high heat. Add beef and cook until browned. Add onion and carrots, reduce heat, and cook some more. Don't forget to stir. Add onions and cook until golden brown. Stir in garlic, add water, and over high heat, heat until boiling. Skim off any gross yellowish-brownish fatty stuff. Stir in tomatoes, reduce heat to low, cover, and let cook another hour, give or take a few minutes depending on whether there's something good on TV. Call daughter-in-law. Ask her whether she's planning to come to Philadelphia for a visit any time soon. Add cabbage, salt and pepper, and bay leaf. Simmer another hour. Call daughter-in-law again, this time because you forgot to tell her that Aunt Shirley never got a thank-you note from her for the books she gave Sam. Add lemon juice and brown sugar, and cook over low heat for fifteen minutes. Finally, the trick: the gingersnaps! Stir them in. Taste. Call daughter-in-law one more time, because you forgot to ask her what Sam wants for his birthday coming up in just seven months. His own computer, perhaps?

Remove the ribs. Cut meat into small pieces and return to the pot.

My next-door-neighbor, Janet, also gave us food. Janet was wonderful. Just for starters, even though she's a doctor, and hence had something to talk about other than dirty diapers, her real passion was food. She gave us a delicious chicken dish, which she served with noodles and a salad. She later gave me the recipe:

1 bottle white wine
Soy sauce
Honey
O.J.
1 chicken, cut up
Pitted prunes
1 package dried egg noodles

Chill wine. When chilled, open bottle and drink. While drinking, combine soy sauce, honey, and O.J. Dump over chicken parts, along with pitted prunes, in a baking dish. Bake at 350 degrees for a while. Make egg noodles according to the package instructions.

Whoops! That's *not* the meal she made for us when we brought our twins home. She made something even better, something she called chicken casanova, with capers and lemon and olive oil and wine and little chopped-up black things, but then again, she's a way better cook than I am. She is, in fact, one of those an-

noying people for whom cooking is a hobby bor-
dering on an obsession, and thus, after she came
home from a day at the hospital spent saving
people on the brink of death, she'd cruise into her im-
possibly well-outfitted cucina and whip up a little
bouillabaisse or homemade ravioli stuffed with herbed
porcini parmesan, while across the driveway we shared,
ensconced in my own kitchen, I'd be working on
canned tuna fish with Hellman's. What I'm trying to
say is that the above meal is the one I made for *her*
when she brought her second child home. By then I'd
learned how important it is to feed people, especially
people who have just given birth. I'm hardly a world-
class cook, but Janet said that the chicken I made for
her was delicious, and thanked me for it.

TWO

The Six-Minute Supper

 A FEW WEEKS AFTER THE *BRIS,* I had a second little psychic meltdown, this one involving the sudden insight that I wasn't cut out for motherhood. Things were pretty desperate in my house: Grandma Lola's cabbage soup was long gone, and my husband, claiming that someone had to pay the bills, had gone back to his regular long hours at work. But at least it was autumn, and the school year had started up again. One morning while Sam was in Pre-K, the twins simultaneously fell asleep. This gave me the opportunity to plonk myself down on the living room sofa, call my mother, and blame her for my own ineptitude.

But again she was cheerful and straightforward. Again she told me that I'd feel better if I got off the sofa and into the kitchen. She said that once I learned that I could "cope" with my new, expanded family, I'd feel what she called "more competent." Naturally I took this so-called advice as not-so-hidden criticism. Why? Because it *was,* that's why. No, I'm NOT being "overly sensitive." Why do you hate me? Which is just one of the many reasons that I'll probably be in psychotherapy for the rest of my life, and I still won't have multiple orgasms. Whatever they are. Meanwhile, I was still so large that the two or three times that I'd managed to get out of the house, total strangers had come up to me and said: "New baby coming soon, huh?"

"Make something hot and nourishing," Mom advised, while I played with the layers of flab on my stomach. But I was diverted from this engrossing activity by the sound of the mail dropping through the slot. It was the distinct *flllpppgggingg* sound of a fat envelope slapping onto the floor. I knew from long experience what it was: another one of my beloved short stories rejected by another editor at another literary magazine somewhere in the Midwest.

"Once you start feeling sorry for yourself," Mom chirped on her end of the phone, "you lose confidence."

I dragged the phone over to the front door, where, sure enough, one of my own manuscripts was waiting for me. I tore open the envelope and the rejection slip, which I've taken the liberty of deconstructing, fell out.

It said: *Isn't it time you stopped writing and started doing something useful, like, just to take a random example, learning to make your own chicken stock?*

"When you start to feel low," Mom was saying, "you need to take ten deep breaths, and remind yourself that you have three beautiful, healthy children and a darling husband."

Perhaps. On the other hand, maybe it was time to face the depressing truth. In short, that I'd become what I'd always dreaded becoming: a harassed and sleep-deprived mother of three verging on middle age with stretch marks and cellulite and a Ford Taurus station wagon with dual-side airbags who despite her earlier visions of herself as a way-cool artistic type living in a garret in Paris had morphed into a woman with nothing more enlightening to do than whine about dust bunnies and who's lucky that her husband ISN'T off boinking other women—women who, after all, don't sit around the house all day in their nightgowns wondering whether they'll ever have a chance to be interviewed on NPR.

"You don't have to do anything complicated," Mom continued. "A simple roast chicken with mashed potatoes and a tossed salad couldn't be easier. Or if that's too much, make spaghetti. Jennifer, Jennifer. Hello? Are you there, Jennifer?"

But I couldn't answer, because by now I'd opened a second piece of mail—a letter from my friend, Melanie. I knew Melanie from school, where we both had wanted to grow up to be writers. At that time, Melanie was talented and blonde and struggling to make art. And in the years since, she hadn't changed much: She was still talented and blonde and struggling to make art. The only difference, according to her letter, was that she was about to have her first novel published by Random House. *Random House?* I prayed that her book would not be reviewed anywhere; that it would die an ugly, unappreciated death; that stacks of it would be remaindered off and finally given, in bulk, to old-age homes. I was so disturbed by Melanie's good news that I think I may have groaned.

"It's not as bad as all that, dear," Mom said. "You can always buy those wonderful already-made fresh tortellinis in the supermarket. I mean, is that easy, or is that easy?"

How should I know? I was beginning to hyperventilate.

"Are you still there, Jennifer?" Mom finally said.

Was I still there? I didn't know. Whereas once—not so long ago—I'd lived in a walk-up apartment in New York, and hung out with wretchedly self-impressed young men who wanted to have sex right there and then on the double mattress on the floor—the same one where they hadn't changed the sheets for months—my new province was the supermarket. The dry cleaners. The pediatrician's office. Not to mention the kitchen. And my husband, who had once *been* one of those young men with the mattress on the floor, and who used to sit around talking about Wittgenstein, for God's sake—and I used to *listen* to him, *that's* how much I liked him—was now a lawyer at an enormous downtown law firm who came home and said, "What's for dinner?" and then proceeded to sigh and tell me about federal trade regulations as they pertained to the antitrust laws in Missouri.

"I don't feel well," I said.

"To tell you the truth," Mom said, "I haven't been feeling so well myself. I've had a lot of pain in my lower areas."

"Jesus, Mom. Do I really have to hear this?"

At this point you are probably saying: Why has this chick been in therapy most of her adult life? Why is she so angry? Why is she so rude to her mother, who has never been anything other than sweet, giving, and loving? Why can't she listen to her mother-in-law, when her mother-in-law tells her that she would catch more flies with honey than with hostility? Was she the victim, perhaps, of long-repressed psychosexual abuse? And if that's the case, then why *didn't* her therapist give her mood-altering medication, like she requested? Has she ever been on *Sally?*

Actually, I had to take a sabbatical from therapy during the first few weeks after Rose's and Jonathan's birth, which was just one more reason that I was losing my mind. And then, for reasons too complicated to get into on this page, I stopped going altogether. By the time this happened, I couldn't help but notice that my psychotherapist was spending more and more time dropping her kid off at my across-the-street neighbor's house, which happened to be across the street. I mean, this was weird. But there is a simple explanation for this seemingly bizarre, counter-psychotherapeutic behavior: Namely, some months *after* I'd already started seeing my psychotherapist and long after I'd become completely dependent on my screaming and sobbing sessions with her, my psychotherapist met and became friendly with my across-the-street neighbor—unaware, at the time, that my across-the-street neighbor lived across the street from me and was, in addition, the mother of Sam's hero—and by the time my psychotherapist found out that her new best friend lived across the street from me, it was too late: Her kid and my neighbor's kid had bonded, the result being that my therapist's kid had play dates within earshot of my kitchen. Mind you, this was the exact same therapist who had pointed out to me on innumerable occasions that she is better than I am, because she, unlike me, had a career and also had a family. Sorry: That's my own paranoid and hostile interpretation of my therapist's many long silences. What I'd *meant* to say is that this particular therapist—the one whose car I kept seeing cruising up my street—was also the one who explained that I have what are called "border issues" to do with my mother who was always dropping by my house because she just happened to be in the neighborhood and she just wanted to see her grandchildren in order to make sure that they hadn't been starved to death or anything lately—bringing a two-quart fish stew casserole with her, just in case.

I began to whimper.

"Look Jennifer," Mom was saying on her end of the line. "I'd really like to help you, but I just can't right now."

"Huh?" I said.

"I'll call you in a little while." she said. "You'll be fine."

Despite how angry I was that my mother hadn't volunteered to come over to my house and make enough pot roast to last until all three of my children had graduated from medical school, I shlepped on down to my kitchen and looked around. Okay, I thought. This is *it*.

Amazingly, within a few weeks, I realized that Mom had been right. I was—just as my mother had predicted—fully capable of producing some sort of edible foodstuffs around dinner time. In fact, I'd been doing it already, only I just didn't know how really good I was at it. The following, then, are the recipes that I developed (some are original to me, others have been passed down) for producing a meal in six minutes or less. Again, I record them in the spirit of full disclosure: my recipes, myself.

Pommes de Terre à Mush

Ingredients: baking potatoes, various vegetables, cheese, baked beans.

Place three or four baking potatoes in a microwave-safe dish and nuke on one side. While nuking, wash and chop any or all of the following ingredients: broccoli, mushrooms, scallions. Run upstairs and threaten to lock Sam in his room if he continues to pull the feathers out of the down quilt that your sisters and brother gave you as a wedding present. At the sound of the beeping microwave, run downstairs, open microwave door, and turn potatoes over. Burn fingertips. Curse and run cold water over fingertips. While second side is being nuked, open can of baked beans and chop up some cheese. Better yet, open the bag of pre-grated cheese that you bought even though it costs more than the un-pre-grated kind. Stick pacifier in Rose's mouth. Watch as pacifier falls on the floor. When potatoes are thoroughly cooked, take them out, slice open, and mash innards. Run water over dirty pacifier. Place other ingredients atop potatoes, return to microwave, and push a few more buttons. Ignore voice of Inner Mother telling you that your husband, like hers, would prefer a steak or a roast chicken. Think about tossing a salad, but don't. Eat when ready.

Mom's "Barbecued" Chicken

Ingredients: store-bought barbecue sauce, onions, chicken pieces, egg noodles.

Broil chicken on both sides until skin is crisp. Do not heed voice in head that tells you that chicken skin is 100 percent fat and if you took the skin *off* you could have ice cream for dessert, because the fact is that you're going to have ice cream for dessert anyway. Who the fuck cares that you decided *before* you were married that you were going to keep kosher? You think God cares? You think He even knows about you, and your kids, and your narcissistic belief that if life were fair, you, rather than Julia Roberts, would be a famous and rich movie star? While chicken is broiling, chop up some onions and open jar of barbecue sauce. When chicken is crisp, drain excess fat. Set oven to bake at 350 degrees. Dump jar of sauce and chopped onions atop chicken, spreading evenly. Cook for about an hour. When chicken is cooked, remember that you meant to make the egg noodles.

Lemon Chicken

Ingredients: lemon, chicken.

Place chicken in pan, breast side up. Push hair back behind ears. Discover that hair is coated with disgusting white liquid slime. In bathroom mirror, observe the way the slime has trickled all the way down back of your sweater. Discard sweater. Toss into corner. Return to kitchen. Wash lemon, pierce with fork, and place in chicken's cavity. Bake at 350 degrees for about an hour. When cooked through, retrieve lemon from cavity, and squeeze the juice over the chicken. Serve with rice and salad, if you happen to have rice and salad. When husband looks at you funny, burst into tears.

Mom's Brisket

Ingredients: brisket, dried ginger, various root vegetables, water, cream-style horseradish.

Discover large, lumpish cut of beef in freezer. Think back to 1989, when you bought it: Is it a brisket or a pot roast, and what's the difference? Call Mom. As she explains that a pot roast usually has a kind of hump, while a brisket tends to be slablike (think of corpses; think of *The Jungle*), cut her off, telling her that you can't talk because the baby, one or the other of them, needs to be changed. How can you tell? Because it *stinks,* that's why. After all, it's really her fault that you're stuck here, amid screaming infants and dirty diapers, because when you were little you wanted to be just like her, and she encouraged you in that direction: the dress-up chest, the Little Suzy Homemaker oven. And now look at you: waiting on your husband, just as your mother waited on Dad. Mom sitting at the kitchen table, looking tired. Where was Dad? Oh yeah—at the office. Where the hell's *your* husband? Oh yeah—at the office. Do men still have affairs with their secretaries? Repress thought.

When Mom again begins to describe her gas pains—or whatever they are—tell her that you don't want to hear about the bomb in her side any more. Tell her that you have to go. Hang up phone. Change diapers. On your way back to the kitchen, decide that the lump of frozen meat is a brisket. Defrost it. When defrosted, coat with ginger. Place in large, heavy pan in half-inch of water. Place onions, potatoes, carrots, and any other vegetables that might possibly taste good around brisket. Bake at 350 degrees uncovered, for an hour or two, maybe three, who knows? Serve with horseradish.

Chicken Salsa

Ingredients: chicken pieces, canned black beans or kidney beans, salsa, onions.

Wash and skin chicken. Or don't. Whatever. You're too tired to make these decisions. Wonder why it is that the song, "I love you, you love me, we're a happy family," sung by Barney the purple dinosaur on TV to the tune of "This Old Man," makes you catatonic with rage. Storm upstairs and pull plug on television. Threaten Sam with being locked in his room. Tell Sam that Barney isn't a dinosaur, he's a whinosaur, and that, actually, he's neither, because what he is is a man dressed in a stupid suit. Say: I hate Barney. Say: If you watch even one more minute of TV, you'll turn into a rock. Cry. Turn TV back on. Return to kitchen. Chop up some onions. Cry some more. Chop up some other stuff—scallions, carrots. Is there *anything* fresh in your "fresh vegetables" drawer? Dump vegetables, canned black beans, and jar or two of salsa on chicken. Sprinkle with black pepper. Compose new lyrics to the "I Love You" song: "I hate you, you hate me, we all live in misery." Realize that you have lost your sense of humor, your biting wit, perhaps forever. Bake, covered, at 350 degrees, until done, about an hour.

Orzo with Cheese and Lima Beans

Ingredients: orzo, grated Parmesan cheese, frozen lima beans, olive oil, fresh minced garlic.

Tell your husband that although this dish may sound gross, it's actually not bad. Tell him that he's lucky to get dinner at all, and if he wants, he can just skip the whole damn thing. Who needs *him?* Go to liquor cabinet. No Scotch. Settle for the one can of Bud hibernating in the back of the fridge. Open Bud. Remember that first weekend of your freshman year of college when you and your roommate went to that frat party and got drunk on lukewarm Bud and you went upstairs to this thick-necked frat boy's room and—well, never mind. Sing: "Tonight, tonight, let it be Löwenbräu."

While singing, cook about a pound of orzo in a large pot of boiling water. Drain. Nuke frozen limas. In large, heavy skillet, sauté garlic in olive oil on low heat. Add limas, orzo, and Parmesan cheese. Stir whole shebang together, turn around to answer ringing phone, and knock skillet off stove and onto floor.

Orientalish Pasta Salad

Salad ingredients: pasta, canned tuna, frozen peas, scallions, other assorted veggies, shelled peanuts.

Dressing: white vinegar, sesame oil, soy sauce, ginger, Dijon mustard.

Gaze at rings on your left hand. Remember how, when you were single in New York and men made rude remarks to you on the street, you'd dream about the day your boyfriend would put an engagement ring on your finger. Those trips with your friend, Megan, to Tiffany's—how the diamonds sparkled under glass. And so, my friend, it comes to this: Orientalish pasta salad for the kabillionth time. Boil water in large, heavy pot. When water boils, dump a box or so of spaghetti in. When done, drain, rinse with cold water, and set aside.

Microwave one box of frozen peas, or peas and carrots. Chop up scallions, avocado, broccoli, red pepper, and any other vegetables that happen to be lying around *sans* mold. Open can of tuna fish.

Combine salad ingredients in large bowl.

Mix dressing ingredients together in another bowl,

going heavy on the vinegar and the ginger. Taste-test with finger. Add a little more of this, a little more of that. Pour over salad and toss. Trip over the "bouncy bounce" in which Jonathan had been sitting, cooing happily, toppling him face-first onto floor. Scoop now-screaming baby boy up, checking for hemorrhages. Call doctor.

Serve cold or at room temp.

My Old Old Boyfriend's Kosher Chicken Kiev with Spinach

Ingredients: skinned, boneless chicken breasts, eggs, plain bread crumbs, margarine, fresh or frozen spinach, toothpicks.

Why did you ever go out with him, anyway? I mean, other than the fact that he had enough dough to buy the entire city of New York? Come to think of it, why did you ever break up? Did you lose your mind, or what?

Detach Rose from left breast and burp her. Answer phone. What do you know? It's not, after all, the fiction editor of the *New Yorker* telling you that the story you sent him three months ago is brilliant, they can't wait to run it, you must be the next Saul Bellow, only with ovaries. It's Mom. Tell her, in your most snootily adolescent voice, that it's a bad time. Say: If you don't feel well, go to the doctor. Say: Or take an aspirin. Say: What does Dad know? Say: Dad's a lawyer,

not a gynecologist. Say: Then get a second opinion. Say: I can't hear you. Sorry, but I can't *hear*
you. Say: She's screaming in my ear. Say: She just
barfed all over me. Hang up. Wipe spit-up off shoulder. Put baby down. Stick pacifier in her mouth. Ignore
screams.

Stick pacifier in Jonathan's mouth. Ignore screams.

Tell Sam that he can *too* wipe his own behind.

Cook spinach, then set aside. Whisk eggs in bowl.
Dip each chicken piece in egg, then in bread crumbs.
Place hunk of margarine and dollops of spinach inside
each breast, and then roll. Fasten with toothpicks and
bake at 350 degrees for fifteen minutes, maybe more,
you decide.

Broccoli, Carrots, and Rice

Ingredients: several heads of cut-up broccoli florets,
several heads of garlic, carrots, olive oil, rice.

Wash broccoli and carrots, and chop up into bite-
sized pieces. Mash up a bunch of garlic. When doorbell
rings, wonder who it is. The UPS man? A person deliv-
ering flowers to you from your husband? Or perhaps a
robber, come to force his way into the house, tie you
up, rape and torture you, and then take off with the silver cutlery you got for your wedding and have never
used? Open door. Say: Hi Dad. Say: What are you doing here at this time of day? Tell him that you're trying
to get dinner on the table. Say: Mom's having *tests?*

What kind of *tests?* Say: Sam's upstairs playing with his Ninja Turtles.

Wonder what kinds of tests would take all afternoon. While Dad goes upstairs to say hi to Sam, retreat into kitchen. When did it get so cold out? And what on earth is Dad doing here, when he's supposed to be at the office? True, he and Sam adore each other in this completely exclusive, puppy-love way—having bonded when Dad taught Sam, then a baby, how to say "grandfather" in Hebrew. Even so, this visit makes no sense. Dad never "drops by," never "hangs out." The concepts don't even apply to him.

Place vegetables, garlic, and some olive oil in a pot, along with a cup or so of water. Bring water to boil. Turn down heat, cover pot, and steam about three minutes. When vegetables are bright-green and tender, remove from heat.

When Dad comes downstairs, say: I still don't get why you're here. Say: Only Mom would tell you to leave. Say: I know she *told* you to visit Sam, but she *meant* that you should stay with her. Roll your eyes. What a relationship.

You have a stomachache. After Dad leaves, lie down on the sofa. When Sam comes downstairs complaining of starvation, make him a peanut butter and jelly sandwich.

Chicken à la Herbs

Ingredients: whole chicken, herbes provençales mixture (available at many gourmet stores).

Wash chicken. Trip over Sam, sprawled out on kitchen floor playing with Ninja Turtles. Reflect on the fact that your child, your own flesh and blood, is fixated on Ninja Turtles. Wonder what's next. G.I. Joes? Video games? Toy uzis? Keg parties? Pot? Girls? Coat chicken with herbs. Worry about Mom. Watch, with mounting, low-level anxiety, as both twins' faces contort with rage. Ignore ensuing screams. Suppress worries about Mom. Her blood tests showed no abnormality, and at her age, all kinds of minor problems can happen. You have other things to worry about, anyway. On way to refrigerator, where you think you may have a bottle of formula, trip again over Sam. Tell him that you are not, under any circumstances, going to buy him a Ninja Turtle video. Tell him he can cry all he wants. Tell him that big boys don't have temper tantrums over Ninja Turtle videos. Threaten to lock him in his room.

Locate bottle of formula. Locate bottle of vodka.

Remember that you chose this life.

Locate clean glass. Pour vodka in.

Apologize to Sam. Tell him that you're not, after all, going to lock him in his room. Wipe his tears. Kiss his cheeks.

Pick up Rose.

Pick up Jonathan.

Pick up Sam.

Rock, in rocking chair, until quiet.

When husband comes home, remember the uncooked chicken.

Call pizza parlor.

THREE

The Chemotherapy Weight Loss Diet

 ONE GORGEOUS BRIGHT FALL DAY when the sky was so blue that it looked like an overhead lake and the leaves were falling in heaps of gold, red, and yellow, my father called to tell me that the kinds of medical tests that take all afternoon were leading to additional tests. These tests, in turn, led to additional tests, and so forth and so on, until, one afternoon in early November, my mother woke up from surgery at Georgetown University Hospital, to discover that she was no longer living in the land of the well. The bomb in her side wasn't—as one of her doctors had suggested—indigestion. It was a malignant tumor, and it was big.

Here's a short, descriptive episode that captures the

side of my mother that I like best: One day when I was sitting in her hospital room, and through the tubes that were stuck every which way into her body, my mother said: "I have an idea for you. Why don't you write a book called 'The Chemotherapy Weight Loss Diet'?" The book, she said, should include recipes for foods that patients who are sick as dogs with nausea can stomach, like won ton soup, and flat ginger ale, and Triskets, and saline solution administered via IV. She said that if I wrote this book, I'd finally be a published writer, and then she wouldn't have to listen to me whine anymore about what a failure I am. And a few days later, in the middle of the night, she went into some kind of psychotic episode from all the painkillers she was on and ripped out all her tubes. The following morning, my father called me to tell me that my mother may have suffered, quote, "brain damage." "They're doing a brain scan now," he said.

I ran into the bathroom and vomited, and then I called my husband, in hysterics. My younger sister called from Los Angeles, sobbing because her children were never going to know their grandmother; then my brother called from the hospital, where he'd been sitting by Mom's side, to say that Dad had been on the phone all afternoon and, in his opinion, had gone over the edge. My older sister called from New York, crying because even though she was single and wasn't really in any great hurry to be anything else, she could no longer stand Mom's incessant worrying that she'd never get married, and was therefore tempted to marry the first loathsome joker to come along, just to put Mom's mind at ease. So we were all calm and cool

about my mother's illness, which is an important trait to have when someone is sick.

A month later, Mom started chemotherapy. And even though her own father had died, of cancer, in 1958, it was as if cancer, and cancer treatments, simply didn't exist for our family, because, and this is the important point: In our family, we don't get sick. True, my father slept in my mother's hospital room for a week. And true, Mom lay in bed begging for painkillers. But in our family, sickness was for other people—inferior, complaining people with poor hand-and-eye coordination, or shallow suburbanites who watched soap operas, or Chinese stowaways. To wit: To get sick in our family simply wasn't *done*.

Yes, there was some denial going around, but only because, in our family, if you don't talk about it, it goes away. Which may be one reason that my father went on a business trip a couple of weeks after Mom finished her first round of chemotherapy, which she was sure was going to be—like childbirth itself—"a snap." I was with her when she started the chemo. She sat upright in her hospital bed, wearing a pretty nightgown, and reading a back issue of *Vanity Fair*, the one with the naked and pregnant Demi Moore on the cover. "Really, Jennifer," she said. "This is going to be a piece of cake. I'm *glad* your father has his work to keep him busy.

Why should he sit around the house all day with nothing to do?" On the bed next to hers, an ancient black woman, her face nearly covered with the bed sheets, groaned.

Mom went home, became dehydrated, lay on the sofa, and waited for her hair to fall out. Gradually the misery of her first round of chemo began to subside. Which was when I invited my mother and my aunt over for dinner. I had this dopey idea that if only Mom ate something nutritious and spent some time with her grandchildren, everything would be—if not hunkydory—then at least *better*. Plus my brother, who lived with his wife and daughters in the rival all-Volvo neighborhood to mine in upper Northwest Washington, had already taken the initiative and had had my mother over for dinner several days earlier. *Well,* I thought, when Mom told me about it, *goody-goody for them.* If they could do it, then I could too.

The truth is, Mom was so sick that not a one of us had any real grasp of what she was facing. Certainly not the two people Mom's illness affected most. After all, Dad had gone out of town on business, and what's more, Mom—like a woman in a bad country western song—had *told* him to. Which was why my aunt was in town. She had flown in from her home in Boston to help out. And the whole thing was, in a word, fucked. Because why was Mom giving Dad permission to pack his briefcase when she was so sick? And why was this same woman—who had always been so disgustingly healthy that I sometimes wanted her to just go away already and leave me *alone*—undergoing chemotherapy, which is what people do for months and months of agony before they die? And why—through all this—did I even *care* when I got rejection slips from pretentious literary magazines in Indiana with names like *The Review of Contemporary Belles Lettres* and *Lit Rag* that no one even *read?* And meanwhile, I thought, why did she have to go and get cancer *now,* when I needed her so much?

In any event, the night that Mom and my aunt were coming to dinner was cold and wet. I was alone in the house with the children, when I sniffed something, turned around, and noticed that my oven had burst into flames. The children and I stared, transfixed, as gray vapors rose up out of the burners on the stove. "Hmm, that's odd," I thought. Then there was this *whooshing* sound, a cross between an explosion and an echo, and through the little window on the oven door I saw bright orange flames. "Cool, Mom," Sam said. "Is our house going to burn down now?"

"Ooops," I thought. The night before, while I'd been up nursing the twins, I'd watched a hospital drama on TV, and one of the patients on it was a burn victim. The guy looked *bad.* Even so, the cute lady doctor who in real life couldn't have been more than twenty-two, and probably had the IQ of a turtle, fell in love with him. And then it turned out that *she* had breast cancer. I was thinking about this show and won-

dering, briefly, whether Mom would skip chemotherapy and go straight to suicide if the children
and I all burned to death, when at last what was
left of my common sense got the better of me and I
turned off the oven and let the flames die out.

"Now what?" I asked Sam.

"How about McDonald's?" he suggested.

First I tried turning the oven back on, but when the
smoke again began to rise, I realized that this wasn't
such a good idea. I didn't know what to do. I mean,
other than scream at Sam, who kept insisting that Mc-
Donald's was his favorite restaurant, and that, moreover, Grammy had promised to take him there as soon
as she felt better. "When are *you* going to take me to
McDonald's? You *never* take me to McDonald's," he
said. At which point I had to threaten to put him in
Time-Out until he was old enough to vote.

The problem was that, when faced with a culinary
disaster, I usually called my mother. In fact, via massive doses of psychotherapy, I was gradually learning
that food was one of the subjects we can discuss without any undercurrent of mother-daughter *mishegoss*.

Here's an illustration of what I mean: If Mom advised me to, for example, "cook it at 350 for a half an
hour or so," all I would *hear* was, "Cook it at 350 for a
half an hour or so," which in turn would allow me to
say something mature, such as: "Okay." But if Mom, to
give a different kind of example, said something along
the lines of: "How is Sam adjusting to all-day pre-K?"

what I would hear was, "Don't you think nine-to-three is an awfully long day for him? When you were Sam's age, you only went to half-day pre-K. What kind of wretched excuse for a mother are you?" Then I'd become defensive and say something really *really* mature, such as: "You never even tried to understand me, did you, Mom?"

But calling Mom, obviously, was out. And the thing is, I really wanted to make Mom a nice dinner—a dinner so delicious, so warm, so nourishing, that all those cancer cells that were swimming around her body would sit up and think twice. And how many nice dinners had she made for *me* over the years—eight, nine billion? Whereas I have rarely cooked for her, and then not with great success, and *never* have I made homemade angel food cake covered with chocolate frosting, still my favorite, and then presented her with a nearly two-foot-tall Babar with a removable red velvet cape and a real crown made of gold. How many times had she nursed me through the flu? How many cups of hot chocolate had she made for me? How many bowls of homemade soup?

It's hard for me to talk about my mother, because every time I do, I get tangled up in the contradictions of her personality, and the web of love and desire and guilt and lack of resolution that has always existed between us, and I lose my bearings. I know that it could take a lifetime for me finally to get a hold of her—to see her clearly, as she is, rather than as she is in relation to me, her second daughter: For I was passionately tied to her in childhood; my love for her felt like my link to life itself. The facts are these: She was born in 1932 to beautiful, wealthy German Jews. She was raised in Scarsdale, New York, excelled in sports, and when she was a teenager, met and fell in love with my father, a Dartmouth man from Baltimore. He was athletic, determined, smart, and handsome, with curly, prematurely graying hair and considerable charm. My mother's sister, Jane, once told me that at first he barely took any notice of her. In November 1956, while my father was on Thanksgiving leave from the navy, my parents were married, in Scarsdale. In the wedding album, my mother is small, dark, pretty, and fragile, with a large smile on her face. He looks out at the camera with a steady, assured gaze. She had never known real unhappiness. In 1958, when my mother's beloved father, Clarence, died of cancer, she was pregnant with me.

And now my mother had the same disease that had killed her father, my house was filled with smoke, my kids were crying, and no matter how often I went around the house saying, "Mom has cancer, Mom has cancer, Mom has cancer," I still didn't understand what it meant. *Mom. Cancer.* The words made no sense.

In a last-ditch effort to save dinner, I called my next-door-neighbor, Janet, who, thank God, was home. "I'll be right over," she said. I threw the two babies into their playpen, and, while Sam watched over them, ran, with Janet by my side, next door to her kitchen, where she took my prepared but not-yet-cooked dishes and put them in her oven, which I happened to notice was, like the rest of her house, clean.

This is what I was making: Vaguely Spanish Chicken; grilled vegetables; green beans; black beans; salad; rice. And I want to talk about the grilled vegetables first, because it was they that caused the fire. What you DON'T want to do, when making grilled vegetables, is to start wondering whether your mother is going to be around long enough to see your kids learn to make pee-pee in the potty, because if you do this, chances are that you'll place your grilled vegetables, sprinkled with olive oil, in the oven on one of those flat cookie sheets that have no sides. And then, five or six minutes after you place the vegetables in the oven and turn the oven on to bake at 400 degrees, the olive oil will drip off the sideless rim of the cookie sheet and onto your heating element, and your oven will explode into flames.

What you DO want to do is this: Slice up some vegetables—the thick, hearty kind that most children refuse to eat, like eggplant and zucchini and rutabaga, and onions and yams, and red and yellow peppers, and just about anything else in your kitchen. Lay them flat on a cookie pan—the kind *with* sides—sprinkle with salt and olive oil, then roast at 400 degrees, *checking often,* until the first side is browned. Remove from oven and turn over. (Different vegetables take longer to cook than others, so keep checking.) Serve the vegetables with black beans, rice, and a side of sour cream, and you've got this absolutely delish meal that also looks really colorful and pretty, and people say, "This is *really good*. How'd you make it?" Black beans are also really easy to make, especially if you do what I do, and buy the Progresso kind in the can, open it, dump the beans into a bowl, and nuke them in the microwave until they're hot.

Even though Janet had rescued the meal, I was in pretty bad shape by the time my husband arrived home. Actually, I'd done something unusually stupid that day, besides almost burn the house down. I'd taken the twins to the pediatrician for their four-month checkup and, while there, had flipped through an entire pile of women's magazines. By the time we were called out of the waiting room and into an examining room, I'd learned (a) that my sex life should be way perkier than it was, and COULD be, too, if only I'd wear a black negligee without panties on underneath when I greeted my husband at the door, but of course I'd never do this, because I am an uptight housewife; (b) that I, too, could learn to stencil my children's furniture and, for mere chump change, create beautiful bedrooms using nothing more than my own ingenuity and a little paint; and (c) many middle-aged women go back to school, and start whole new careers as doctors or college professors, and I could, too, if only I had even an ounce of energy or get-up-and-go. So when my husband, taking off his coat in the entry way, said, "What's for dinner, Jen? It smells like smoke in here," I burst into tears and went screaming into the bathroom.

A few minutes later, my mother and aunt walked in the door, looking oddly like two coeds who'd snuck out of the girls' dormitory to meet their boyfriends at a local bar. Meanwhile the phone rang. It was Janet, calling with a progress report. She'd removed the eggplant and the bell peppers from the oven, but not the rutabaga, and was that okay? "Use your judgment!" I shouted, and slammed down the phone. "Would you like something to drink? Perhaps a glass of wine?" I asked my guests. "No," Mom said, "but it looks like you need something."

Well, yes, I did, and the vodka helped. Twenty minutes later, after Janet called to say that she was worried that the chicken would dry out if it stayed in the oven much longer, I sent my aunt next door to retrieve our dinner, and we all sat down. Amazingly, the meal wasn't any worse for wear, and the slightly smoked flavor that the explosion had given both the chicken and the vegetables enhanced our enjoyment of it. But now I want to talk about the chicken, because the recipe I'd used was one my mother had taught me a long time ago, and during the first summer of my marriage, I made it sixteen, seventeen zillion times. Like so many of her other recipes, its brilliance lies in the fact that it is the culinary equivalent of a complete no-brainer. What you do is dump a bunch of olive oil, canned tomatoes, minced garlic, and ground cumin on chicken pieces, then cook it. You can also add other things, if you happen to have them around, which is what I did—like peas and kalamata olives and some sliced scallions.

Over the years, my mother had taught me many of her kitchen tricks, but by no means all of them. Some secrets have to remain secret, or they lose their potency. I doubt I'll ever be able to make my mother's marinated cucumber salad—the best I've ever tasted—or her apricot torte, or her butterfly of roast lamb. I know I'll never make a duck à l'orange come out the way hers does: juicy on the inside, crispy on the outside, and completely grease free. I mention this dish in particular because it's my favorite, and Mom always made it for me on special occasions, like my birthday or the day my high school guidance counselor called with the good news that I hadn't, after all, flunked physics. Here's the recipe:

Duck à l'Orange à la Mom

    1 8-ounce can frozen orange juice, defrosted
    1 jar currant jelly
    1 duck

Preset oven to broil. Mix orange juice and currant jelly. Wash duck and place in oven, degreasing often, until skin is crispy brown. Remove duck from oven and cover with orange juice mixture. Set oven at 350 degrees and return duck. Cook until done, about two hours, degreasing often. Serve with wild rice and salad.

But Mom was out of commission, and I knew that

she wouldn't be making duck à l'orange any time soon. I tried to tell myself that God really didn't want her, anyway—that she had years and years left on earth to complete her mission and finally send me into the loony bin for real. Plus I didn't think that He, in His infinite wisdom, wanted to see my mother's kitchen turn into the complete disaster area that it surely would be if my father were left in charge of it. The man can't boil water. He can't wash dishes. He can't *sweep.* He is so deeply incompetent domestically that it's a wonder he didn't set the house on fire years ago.

"Marry a man like my father," she told me, over and over again, when I was a girl. Her eyes would fill with tears. "He was so wonderful," she'd say. "So loving, so full of fun, with a twinkle in his eye, and, Jennifer, you would have loved him." She'd hold my hand, squeeze it. "He made everyone happy."

She taught me to do the Charleston and the Lindy Hop, the two of us laughing in the kitchen, our knees jerking in and out; she taught me how to make brownies from scratch, and how to get the lumps out of mashed potatoes. She gave me paints and brushes, dance leotards and music. She loved me, passionately, and when I became zombie-like with depression in high school she sent me to my first psychiatrist. Once, when I'd locked myself in my room, she stood outside the door for hours, begging me to let her in. For my wedding day, she wrote a poem so sweet and so sentimental that all our guests were in tears.

It began to snow. Fat, wet, white snowflakes were falling outside our windows. We sat down to dinner. Mom tried to eat, but couldn't get much in. A few pieces of chicken. A carrot or two. She fiddled with her hair and said:

"They tell me that it's all going to come out at once, in one big clump."

As she and my aunt were leaving, I thought about asking my mother for her recipes—the ones she's concocted over the years but that exist nowhere other than her own head—but then I thought that that would be a touch too maudlin, and she and I would probably sink into this bath of sentimentality and start crying, and we'd have to hash out our entire mother-daughter relationship right then and there, and we'd wind up in mother-daughter therapy, and start going to mother-daughter therapy support group retreats in upstate New York, and my therapist would have to drop me from her roster of patients, so badly had I allowed myself to become re-merged. So instead I smiled and said: "We'll have you for dinner again!" Mom said she'd like that, and then she and my aunt were out the door.

("Marry a man like my father, Jennifer," Mom said over and over. She was thirty, then forty, then fifty, then sixty, and she kept telling me the same thing. Then I met and married my husband—a good, kind, trustworthy man, a man who loved me and only me. And then my mother was sixty-three, sick with the same disease that had killed her father. Sometimes I wonder if,

in some tiny part of herself, she wants to be with him, be where he is. Sometimes I look at his picture—a beautiful black-and-white studio portrait
of a very young, very handsome man wearing a wool
suit and vest and gazing off somewhere in the mid-dis-
tance. What did he see? Sometimes I talk to him: I ask
him to take care of his daughter. I tell him that none of
us have been able to. He looks at me, and past me, and
doesn't say a word.)

FOUR

Road Hogs

FOR OBVIOUS REASONS, I didn't much feel like dancing naked on a table when New Year's Eve approached. Mom was spending more and more time hooked up to an IV. It was cold. I was so tired that every night when I at last fell asleep, I dreamed about taking a nap. And anyway—not that I want to be vulgar—New Year's Eve sucks. Everyone knows this, and yet every year, just about everyone pretends otherwise. It's like a case of mass repression. What's there to celebrate, anyway? That you got through the Hanukkah-Christmas season, with all its attendant forced merriment, without lighting your hair, if you happen not to be in chemotherapy, on fire?

But I shouldn't talk. The truth is that at one time

my husband and I had our own special New
Year's Eve ritual—and like our other little rituals,
it may not be for everyone, but it worked for us.
Like most other private rituals, it took some time until our ritual was fully evolved. Early in our relationship, when my husband was still "that-boy-who-my-
daughter-is-wasting-her-time-with-he-doesn't-even-
own-a-decent-suit-and-God-knows-if-he'll-ever-make-
a-dime-he's-still-in-school-the-last-one-was-better," we
actually put on New Year's Eve clothes—me in a
swishy black number, he in a tux—and went to a gala
ball in a shopping mall. We drank the kind of cheap
champagne that tastes like beer with NutraSweet in
it and sat next to a recently divorced middle-aged
woman named Judy who asked my husband to go
home with her and tuck her into bed. Our table was
located next to a shoe store, the windows of which
were filled with the neo-Edwardian boots that were
then in style. Talk about depressing. Afterward, my
husband and I went back to his extremely filthy student apartment and got into a big fight about what a
total jerk he was.

But after we got married and produced Sam, our ritual changed. Now what we did was: sit around the
house, analyzing the faults and foibles of our relatives.
Then, around ten o'clock, one of us would mention the
bottle of cheap champagne in the refrigerator that our
realtor had given us when we bought our house. My
husband would say: "It's still *in* there." And I'd say:

"So?" And he'd say: "Come on. It's New Year's Eve." And I'd say: "I'm tired. I'm going to bed." And he'd say: "What about a little New Year's love?" And I'd say: "You've got to be kidding."

But for some reason that still makes no sense to me, the year our twins were born and my mother got sick, we thought we might try something different. This year our usual ritual was out of the question, because we were too tired even to remember the bottle of cheap champagne in the back of the refrigerator. We were too tired to remember one another's names, let alone remember the names of all our relatives, who in previous years had inspired us to such conversational heights. We were too tired, in fact, to do much of anything other than worry about my mother and change an occasional diaper.

Then my husband, who was spending far too many hours sitting in front of a computer, and hence was suffering under the delusion that I was, more often than not, awake, announced that we should have a New Year's Day Open House. My husband has all these dumb ideas about "entertaining." I don't know where he gets them. I think from my mother, who, before she got sick, did things like invite twenty people over for dinner on the spur of the moment. He said: "Jen, why don't we have a few people over on the first of the year?" And I said: "Forget it." And he said: "It doesn't have to be any big deal. We never entertain anymore." And I said: "If you want to entertain, you should have married Martha Stewart." And he said, "If she's feeling up to it, your mother could come. She loves parties." And I said, "Then you should have married *her*."

It was a nice idea. But I knew we wouldn't really be giving a New Year's Day Open House and that even if we did, Mom wouldn't have the strength to attend. What she *would* have the strength to do was: lie on the sofa under an old quilt, with an IV stuck in her arm. Although Mom kept saying that she was "hanging in," any idiot could see that in just a few weeks, she'd lost about twenty pounds, and her skin was the color of a moldy newspaper.

Even so, I found myself consulting my old copies of *Bon Appetit* magazine, which I'd acquired five years earlier when I was, briefly, a *Bon Appetit* staffer, and still under the impression that I had a life. I'm referring to the last job I had before Sam was born, after which I'd retired to my home to become a "full-time" borderline schizophrenic. I was the only person on the staff of *Bon Appetit* who didn't know diddly about food, and I didn't exactly endear myself to the food people (the staff was divided, roughly, into food people and word people). Every time I went ahead and edited a recipe— which for some unnecessary reason was a part of my job description—I made little boo-boos, like substituting the word *boil* for the word *oil*, or *mints* for *mince*, or *masturbate* for *macerate*.

So there I was, consulting my old *Bon Appetit*s,

chuckling over my memories of the days before I
got pregnant with our first child and started getting sick at the first whiff of roasted chicken with
herbs on a bed of garlic greens from the magazine's test
kitchens—the days when I, despite everything, was a
food-sophisticate-in-training. The days when I could
throw words like *insouciance, infused,* and *exquisite*
around with insouciance. And there I sat, at our
kitchen table in Washington, D.C., getting ideas for
this theoretical New Year's Day Open House, and
wondering at what age (now that my *own* chances of
growing a tumor had more than quintupled) I should
start having routine CAT scans? On one page there
was a picture of something called roast duck with
rhubarb-orange compote. Looked good, *real* good.
Sure I could make that, especially if I were Julia Child.
How about some bittersweet chocolate and fresh mint
truffles? Why the heck not? Or I might even tackle the
chicken liver toasts with sage and parsley. The text advised me to "enjoy these tasty treats on a quiet night
with a loved one." Speaking of which, where the hell
had I put my twins? Weren't they being awfully quiet?

Then my sister Binky—the one who isn't married
and lives in this totally fabulous West Side apartment
with views of Central Park and snot-free living room
upholstery—called. She said: "Read any good books
lately?" Whereupon I burst into tears, because not only
had I not read any good books lately, I hadn't read anything other than the Doctor Spock entry on diaper rash

and a pamphlet called "Ovarian Cancer: How to Spot the Early Warning Signs," and the truth was, and it all came crashing down on me, I would probably never "entertain" again. Then the twins woke up from their nap and began to scream.

By this time Grandma Lola had called from Philadelphia to suggest that we visit her for a few days over the holiday, because, after all, she hadn't seen us in *months,* and she meant *months,* and her grandchildren were growing up not knowing who she was, and by the way had we given any thought to moving closer to her, such as, for example, to Philadelphia? I told her that I was too worried about Mom to do much of anything. But she said: "Oh, Jennifer. I know it's awful, but every dark cloud has a silver spoon in its mouth," and as I sat there trying to figure out what she meant, she said: "Your mother needs you, but *you* need a coffee break." Lola had lost her own husband, my husband's father, Stanley, to cancer, in 1985, so she spoke from experience. In a flash, I realized that she was right. Maybe a little trip wasn't such a bad idea. And even though I was still slightly annoyed with her because the last time she had come to my house she had, in her ongoing efforts to help me, unloaded the dishwasher and put all the dirty dishes away in the wrong places, we decided to go to Philly.

As I was packing for the visit, I started thinking about road trips my husband and I had taken before the children had been born—to places like the Mohonk Mountain House and Lake Arrowhead, where we would eat and eat and talk and talk and make love and sleep late. How much fun we'd had, tootling around the country, eating everything in sight. I was thin, I was young, I could pack everything I needed for a weekend away in about ten seconds. Actually, there was one other thing I was thinking about. Okay, two. Three. For example, there was my husband's girlfriend Martha Stewart, and all the nonsense she foists on womankind during this, easily the most tedious, time of year. Like you're really going to throw a New Year's Day party? Like you're really going to *enjoy* it? Like you're really going to make little home-baked loaves of bread for your friends and relatives? And can your own peaches? And dry your own fucking herbs? True, she might live in this fabulous farmhouse in Connecticut and spend every spare second faux-marbleizing, but in Washington, D.C., it was all I could do to remove my own toe lint.

I was also taking stock. Because I'd come to realize that I looked bad. I looked real bad. It had been months since I'd worn anything other than my husband's college sweatshirt, very comfortable antique running shoes, and a pair of my mother's cast-off stretch pants that she'd given me after I gave birth to Sam, on the theory that I was too flabby even to bother trying to look decent.

Finally, I was thinking about this absolutely fabulous dark chocolate macadamia nut tart that my friend Josephine made for us when Sam was born, but that my mother, who had more or less moved in with us to help, wouldn't let us eat, reasoning that it was too good for us, we had to save it for company. And what, after all, had happened to that tart? Had it moved with us from Los Angeles to Washington? If so, could it, along with the bottle of cheap champagne that our realtor had given us, be hibernating somewhere in the back of our refrigerator? Hidden, perhaps, under some wilted lettuce? And if this were the case, could we take it out now, and have it for New Year's?

It really was an incredible thing. So as soon as we got back from Philadelphia I asked Josephine to send the recipe. Here it is, the recipe along with Josephine's instructions, word for word as she sent it:

Chocolate Mac-Nut Tart

1 9-inch tart shell, lightly baked
8 ounces bittersweet chocolate, chopped into bite-size
    pieces
12 ounces unsalted macadamia nuts
2 handfuls sweetened coconut
Nut cream

Nut Cream
¼ cup butter, melted slightly browned, and cooled
Whisk together and add to butter:
2¼ whole eggs and 2¼ egg yolks

¼ cup sugar
½ cup dark Karo syrup

Sprinkle coconut, chocolate, and nuts on the bottom of baked tart shell, keeping the shell in the pan. Pour nut cream over them. Stick tart pan on cookie sheet; cover sides of tart with tin foil so that it will not burn. Bake at 350 degrees for forty to sixty minutes (I can't remember exactly). Tart is done when filling is firm. (Don't burn the damn thing.) Same principle as in cooking a quiche. Cool. Remove from pan.

P.S. Call me if you need help. Call me anyway.

Could I make this thing? Doubtful. But everything was running together in my brain. And so I once again came to the conclusion that:

Food, it runs our lives.

Finally, I'd finished packing. And the thing about packing for this trip, like the thing about packing for all our other trips, was that *I* did all the packing, while my husband went to the office to "check on my e-mail." Fifteen minutes before we were scheduled to leave, my husband came home, threw his toothbrush, book, and underwear in his gym bag, and said: "What's the hold-up? Let's hit the road already!"

Here's a partial inventory of what I'd packed: Sam's clothes, pj's, toothbrush, Ninja Turtles, crayons, My First Walkman, Raffi tapes, Big Bird tapes, Mr. Blanket, and Willy-Billy, the stuffed tyrannosaurus rex with whom he slept; aspirin, Tylenol, nursing bras, dental floss, extra underwear, nightgown, bathrobe, good clothes in case we went out to dinner, Mom's old black stretch pants, Dr. Spock, ovarian cancer handbook, a book called *The Jewish Way of Death and Dying;* Baby Tylenol, a rectal thermometer, four baby turtlenecks, four t-shirts, eight pairs of socks, two pairs of "Padders," four "onesies," four all-in-one baby outfits, six "bunny suit" sleepers, two packages of Pampers (one girl's, one boy's), four receiving blankets, two packages of disposable bottom wipes, extra bottles, extra nipples, his and hers pacifiers, Doggy, Teddy Bear, a dozen *shmates* (for spit-up), the double stroller, a port-a-crib, two "bouncy bounces," a couple of gallons of formula, and a few cases of Gerber's baby food. Speaking of which, I also had to pack a snack bag.

Food is the single most important thing you can have on a road trip, especially one undertaken in the company of children or one undertaken in the company of any person with a penis. Remember the trips *you* took in the back of *your* mother's station wagon when you were a kid? Remember the combined odors of Welch's grape juice and bologna sandwiches and peanut butter crackers? Your brother hitting you? Your sister reading a Nancy Drew mystery in her place behind the driver's seat and then, just as your mother had predicted, barfing? Your father, who never spoke, *glowering* that intimidating *glower* of his? He could make you pee in your pants, just by looking at you this way. Those blue-green eyes bore right into you, right into your soul. What else did he see? In your early twenties, you actually stopped talking to him. Why? He's never done anything worse than force you to read his op ed pieces in the *Washington Post*. Plus he paid for your shrink.

So here we were, on New Year's Day morning, getting ready for our trip. It was cold. Sam was complaining about the fact that Santa hadn't come to our house. He harangued me so much about Santa's repeated failure to show up that I finally broke down and told him the truth about old Saint Nick, namely, that he is an anti-Semite. We had three hours of road time ahead of us. Fortunately, my husband, who in his youth had been an Eagle Scout, was prepared. He said: "Jen, have you packed food for the car?"

And I said: "Why don't *you* pack food for the car?"

And he said: "Jen, your daughter's got poop in her pants."

So I stormed into the house to change Rose's diaper and, while I was at it, grabbed the bunch of over-ripe bananas that, in my haste, I'd forgotten to pack.

When I got into the car, Sam said "Mom, what's an anti-Semite?" My husband growled something about small pitchers possessing big ears, Sam said, "I do *not* have big ears," and the twins began to cry.

We were ready! Our house was locked, our lights were off, and our car packed to the gills with all this junk. And guess what? It was *not* the same car that my husband and I had tootled around in before our kids

had been born. That car had been an old VW
Rabbit, light blue and rusted around the joints.
It didn't go fast, and it broke down if you used
the air-conditioning, but it had a kind of hip gestalt.
We'd upgraded. Now we were cruising in a Ford Taurus
station wagon with dualside airbags that we had pur-
chased for far too much money, because my husband
and I are both total wimps when it comes to "bargain-
ing." We are, in fact, afraid of hurting the salesman's
feelings by *not* buying from him, when, after all, he'd
just spent upwards of a half-hour accompanying us on
a "test drive" through the shopping mall parking lots.

"Mommy, I'm hungry," Sam said as we pulled out
of our driveway.

Thus I spent New Year's Day turned backward in the
front seat of the car, my rear in the air, trying to pacify
my children with treats from our New Year's Day goody
bag. Though this position rendered me hopelessly nauseated, the trip wasn't a total loss, because—just like in
the old days, when it was just me and my husband and
miles of open prairie—we were able to really talk. For
example, Sam and I had the following conversation:

"I don't like string cheese."

"Do you want an apple?"

"This apple is yucky. I want a cookie."

"We don't have any cookies."

"You never give me cookies."

"That isn't true. You had one yesterday."

"I want one now."

"We don't have any cookies."

"I want a Pop Tart."

"We don't have any Pop Tarts."

"Do you have a vagina?"

Our babies, barely five months old, were hungry too, and so I kept hopping back to give them bottles and watch them spit up. It's a real test of the strength of your marriage to see if you can endure three solid hours of crying in stereo while simultaneously carrying on a conversation about the war in Bosnia. Our children, meanwhile, were less than quiet, and the twins were so clued into one another, in this preverbal twin-connection way, that they almost always shrieked in unison.

"You and your stupid sperm," I told my husband.

"What's sperm?" Sam asked.

"What's sperm?" Sam asked the doorman of the building in Elkins Park, Pennsylvania, where my mother-in-law lives.

"What's sperm?" Sam asked the lady in the elevator, a woman whom I'd never before met, who said: "In my day children were taught how to behave."

"Do you have a vagina?" Sam asked.

It wasn't what we had planned, but in retrospect, it wasn't a bad way to start the New Year. After we had unloaded the car and shlepped all our stuff up to Grandma Lola's apartment, we did what we'd previously barely dared to dream about. Grandma Lola took the children, and my husband and I took a nap.

Cooking for Your Boyfriend

NOT LONG AFTER OUR RETURN from Philadelphia, I noticed that our car was seriously gross. I've personally always been offended by cars that smell of ancient spilled Yahoo and soiled diapers. So one day I went berserk and made my husband clean it, and after he'd cleaned it, we got into this big "discussion" about what a control freak I am and how, in addition, I'm way too old to still be blaming my parents for the fact that I haven't yet written my first, brilliant novel, the one that will prove, once and for all, blah blah blah blah blah, I'm boring even myself to death, plus which, why was I worrying about my career when my mother had this horrible disease that could kill her and was even now lying on the sofa surrounded

by gossip magazines that she couldn't read because she was so sick that she could barely lift her
head from the pillow?

But then, around Valentine's Day, I managed to
squeeze into my old "fat jeans." In my triumph, I began
to feel more hopeful. Maybe, I thought, Mom will get
through this. And maybe, I thought, I *won't* be nothing
more than an extension of my children's needs . . . and
maybe they *won't* all require massive doses of psychi-
atric intervention at some point later in life in order to
recover from having had such a bad mother. Indeed,
despite efforts to the contrary, I had yet to inflict complete psychic damage on Sam. Nor had I done anything
really terrible to my twins, such as drop them on their
heads in the bathtub.

I was in such a good mood after I squeezed back
into my "fat jeans" that when I happened to run into
an old boyfriend, I decided to invite him over for dinner. After all, my mother, who loved to entertain, was
always doing things like that. As she always put it, "It's
no big deal."

Except, for me, it *was* a big deal. First off, this was a
boyfriend whom my husband didn't even know I had
had, which opened up a whole long inquiry that I'm
not going to go into right now, because my husband
still didn't know that, when I was single, I was so flirta-
tious that it's a miracle I didn't end up dead in some incredibly seedy apartment in Staten Island. Second, this
boyfriend—whom I had dated for a few minutes dur-

ing those heady days when I was starting out my brilliant literary career as an assistant at *Mademoiselle,* where my duties mainly included typing up articles about orgasms—had witnessed certain embarrassing moments of mine that no one else, including my various shrinks, knew about and which I'm not going to go into right now. And it turned out that after all these years during which I assumed he was still living in New York because that's what the ex-friend of mine who had originally introduced me to him had told me before he became my ex-friend, he (my boyfriend) was in fact NOT living in New York, but rather, living just a couple of miles down the road from me in Washington, in the same lawyer-dominated neighborhood that my brother lived in. *And,* and this is where it gets really gross, in this small-world, inside-the-Beltway way, my boyfriend, it turned out, had for *five* years been working shoulder to shoulder with my father.

Which meant that my boyfriend knew all about me, except that he couldn't, really, because my father, for whom he had been doing all kinds of dreary shit work, rarely talks, except on occasion to say: "But if I marry *you,* sweetie, we'll have to throw Mommy out." Creepier still was the fact that if he *did* in fact know all about me, and was *still* friends with my ex-friend who had originally introduced me to my boyfriend, then my ex-friend knew all about me too. And this is the kind of ex-friend who definitely shouldn't be on the receiving end of any such gossipy tidbits about you as: "Did you hear about Jennifer? Not that there's any news, because, after all, she 'retired' from her so-called career doing whatever it was she was doing, and is now staying home with the kids, whining." No, you do NOT want your ex-friend to know this about you. Especially if your ex-friend happens to be the CEO of a multimillion-dollar company and is in the midst of decorating a beach house.

Yes. Well. Whew. I'm glad I got that off my chest. Because now I'm ready to describe the meal I made. After consulting my two former college roommates, my across-the-street neighbor who hangs out with my shrink, my shrink, my son Sam's best friend, Nicholas, Nicholas's mom, Karen, my next-door neighbor Janet, Janet's nanny, and my husband, I decided to call my boyfriend and invite him to dinner after all. Because it turned out that my boyfriend was himself married and the father of a little boy, plus which his wife had a second bun in her oven, chances were that he wasn't going to say anything embarrassing at the dinner table about me, the kind of thing it makes me cringe just to think about.

So it was in a spirit of yuppie one-upmanship that I finally issued an invitation to dinner at my house. Let me explain. Life is a competition. Anyone who tells you otherwise is lying. I learned this at the parental knee. Have I mentioned that my family was somewhat competitive? Indeed, I come from the type of family where we children knew what was expected of us. And what was expected of us was that we all go to either

Harvard or Yale, like our smart cousins in
Boston. Fortunately, my parents were realists,
and they recognized early on that I was blessed
with strengths other than academic ones, such as, in
my case, having good hair. And yes! I might not have
gone to Harvard, or even to a lesser branch of Harvard, but to this day I not only have good hair, the
kind of hair that hairdressers coo over, but also, I have
the BEST hair in my ENTIRE family! So put *that* in your
pipe and smoke it, why don't you?

My boyfriend, however, had gone to both an Ivy
League college and an Ivy League law school, not to
mention that he was now working for the same major
league law firm that had put me and my three siblings
through college, making him, arguably, a more "successful" person than I was. His wife, too, had hoity-
toity credentials. I was panicked.

I still had one card left, though. I mean, besides the
fact that despite the fact that I had collected zillions of
rejection slips from literary magazines all over America,
I had decided not to jump off a bridge. To wit: I still
had Mom. She may have been sick, but she wasn't
dead. On my next visit, I asked her what I should make
for dinner. Between trips to the toilet, she gave me her
recipes for: Chicken with Artichokes and Onions
Baked in Clay and: Sweet and Sour Red Cabbage.

And this is why my mother is really cool. Even
though she was so nauseated that she could barely
stomach ginger ale, she went into great detail over the

recipes and finally insisted that I take her entire recipe box, because, in her own words, "When, if ever, am I going to need it again? And God knows your father can't cook worth a damn."

As I drove back home with my mother's precious recipe box beside me, I decided to round out the menu with noodles, green salad in a simple mustard vinaigrette, and wine. For dessert, I'd do something sinfully simple. Something luscious yet easy. Something, in other words, that you can buy. Strawberry sorbet smothered in fresh strawberries.

"I'm looking forward to your coming," I said to my boyfriend on the phone.

But after I hung up, I wondered: Did I make an inadvertent but terrible pun of sexual innuendo? What *had* he and I talked about, so many years ago?

In addition to my mother's fabulous recipes, I had one other winning credential. I had produced TWO— count them, TWO—children in one pregnancy. In my neighborhood, where everything was up for grabs in terms of yuppie oneupsman- or -women-ship, this counts. To be sure, the pregnancy had been a completely wretched experience, marked by nausea, stretch marks, back pain, hemorrhoids, and all the rest of it. True, for a while my husband had referred to me affectionately as "my little gas main." But that was *then,* and this was now, and I was back in my "fat jeans," and no one, least of all my boyfriend, could stop me.

"They're coming, I mean arriving, around seven-thirty," I told my husband. "They're bringing their kid. Be home on time, or I'll kill you."

I had to have a game plan (all the cooking magazines tell you so) because you don't want to have to do everything at the last minute and discover, a few minutes before your little dinner party is supposed to start, that you forgot to go grocery shopping. Check this out: A full day before the event, I went to my neighborhood Safeway, and I even managed to take a list of ingredients with me, so as not to forget, for example, the chicken. Then, on the morning of our fête, while Sam was at school, I made my mother's wonderful sweet-and-sour red cabbage.

My Mother's Wonderful Sweet and Sour Red Cabbage (aka: Glutinous Cabbage)

Ingredients: margarine or butter, red cabbage, white vinegar, brown sugar, apples, flour.

In a large skillet, melt some margarine or butter. Chop up a bunch of red cabbage, and, while you're at it, chop up some apples. Add cabbage and apples to skillet. Then add some water. Cover and simmer on low until cabbage is wilted. Trip over daughter, as she attempts to "combat crawl" across your incredibly filthy floor. Watch with horror as she gasps for breath. Wonder whether you should call your pediatrician, and if so, what do you tell her? "I kicked my daughter in the face?" Decide that pediatrician is sick of hearing from you, and that if your daughter actually begins to convulse, you'll do something. In the meantime, isn't it odd that you're so set on having your ex-boyfriend over for dinner? Are you going to turn out to be one of those awful old women who live continuously in the past, recounting, like Blanche DuBois in *A Streetcar Named Desire,* the glory days of your youth? Or was that some other character, some other play? Great. You can't even keep your major literary events straight any more. A sign of early Alzheimer's? And why is it that for the past decade or so you've been dreaming about doing the do with an elementary school class-mate of yours who was so superior that he wouldn't even talk to you? Maybe you really don't love your hus-band. Maybe you rushed into things, after all. Maybe when your husband gets home you'll tell him about your bizarre recurring dream and share your concerns with him. Then the two of you can go into couples therapy, and get a divorce.

Answer phone. It's your husband, calling to "talk something over with you." Uh-oh. Have you been talk-ing in your sleep? But he isn't calling to confront you about your odd little fantasy life, but rather, to tell you that, with your permission, he's sending his resumé to every decent law school in the country, including to places that you can't even locate on a map, like Al-abama. Sigh. While he talks, take a little trip down memory lane, and while you're at it, ask yourself the following question: Why on earth didn't you see it coming when, during his law school days, he confided to you that his real dream was not to make a pile of dough as a partner at some prestigious law firm but, rather, to get a teaching job? And how would you respond? You'd nod and smile. All that love, obviously, had made you stupid. He'd *meant* it when he'd said he didn't really care about money, moron! He's *never* really wanted to spend his life inside an expensive gray suit. And now he's gone ahead and done up his resumé. He's even writing complicated legal articles with lots of footnotes and references, in a language that is and yet is not standard English. Shit. How much do law professors make? Not to worry, not with all the cash you're pulling in as a writer of short stories that never get published.

Say: Uh-huh, uh-huh.

When he's done, tell him that you understand that he doesn't want to be a lawyer anymore, but all in all, you'd prefer it if his next job was in Washington. Why? Because it took you almost five years to make friends here, you're only now beginning to feel as if you're no longer in quarantine, and you'll be damned if you're going to start all over again. Say: At my age. Say: I know, I know. Say: But there are *zillions* of law schools right here. Say: I'll go anywhere except the South.

When cabbage is sufficiently wilted, add a little vinegar, then a little brown sugar, then a little vinegar, and so on, until it tastes right. Add a tad of flour, to thicken. Notice white slime on floor: Clean it. Notice white slime in hair: Begin to cry. Why do you still cry so much? Perhaps it's time to go back into psychoanalysis. Simmer, on low, for hours and hours, making sure that cabbage doesn't congeal into little clumps of purple glue. Add salt and pepper. Serve warm.

So like I said, I made the cabbage, and it *was* yummy-good. My boyfriend ended up having two helpings.

When he and his wife and kid came, I mean arrived, at our house, around seven-thirty, Sam was practicing his Power Ranger karate moves in the living room, and our twins were bathed and newly diapered and wearing their "bunny suits" (zip-up pj's with feet). My boyfriend's pregnant wife came bearing gifts—board books for the twins and a puzzle for Sam. My boyfriend's two-year-old son smiled and said: "Pleased to meet you." Then we all sat around making nervous small talk, mainly about how hard it is to make partner, even though my husband had come to recognize that he would probably never make partner, but only because he'd decided that, all things considered, he wanted to see what his children looked like awake.

But at least dinner was well under way. Because in addition to the red cabbage, which was simmering aromatically on the stove top, the chicken and the other stuff was underway. As was the table, which I'd set with the "good" china that had been a wedding gift from some clients of my father. It was just like my mother's old dinner parties—*grown-up* dinner parties: The table was pretty, the kids were clean, there was food and wine, and the only thing people were talking about had to do with practicing law. Except of course at my mother's dinner parties, the entrée was *cooked.*

In a minute I will get to the recipe for the chicken with artichokes and mushrooms baked in clay that I've since made a thousand times, and, trust me, it is seriously delish. But for right now, a word or two on cooking in clay. For some reason that I can't fathom, the prospect of cooking in a clay cooker intimidates a lot of otherwise excellent and adventurous cooks. And it shouldn't, because it's easy. The trick with a clay cooker is that you immerse the whole thing in cold water for fifteen or twenty minutes before you stick your ingredients in it. That way the clay itself soaks up the water, and then, during cooking, slowly releases its moisture into whatever is inside. Thus, you practically ensure that your chicken or lamb chops or brisket or whatever is moist and juicy. After you've arranged all your ingredients inside your presoaked cooker, you place the cooker in a cold oven, and *then* set the temperature, usually to around 425 degrees. If you don't start with a cold oven, the clay can freak out, withholding its moisture and voting Republican in the local elections. My mistake, then, was *not* that I forgot this small but vital step, nor was it that I forgot to turn the oven on, nor was it that I blew up the oven, as I almost had in December. My mistake was that I forgot that a week or so earlier, the Sears repair man was making his bimonthly visit to my kitchen, this time to "fix" the "lock" on my oven door that had become permanently locked. He kept fiddling with the on-off and lock-unlock mechanism until, at last, he was able to charge me ninety-three dollars and forty-two cents for the following advice: "I suggest that you be more careful in the future." He had, however, unlocked the lock, and while he was at it, he'd mistakenly taken the nobby-thing off the oven's control panel. He did, however, put it back. How was I to know that he put it back UPSIDE DOWN? So that when I went to set the oven on 425 degrees, I was really setting it on Clean?

What an incredibly dumb chick, you're saying. No wonder she didn't get into Harvaard. She probably can't even spell Harvaard. Why didn't she check to make sure that her chicken was cooking properly? Well, you see, what happened was that, after I composed my chicken and put it in my cooker and placed the cooker in the cold oven, which I then set on Clean, Sam went outside to see if it was snowing yet and, within seconds, disappeared. Okay, I thought. Let's be sensible. He's either (a) lost, (b) lying in the middle of the road, a victim of a hit-and-run accident, or (c) kidnapped by those two men who drove up a few minutes ago in what seemed to be a plumber's truck but is actually a specially designed kidnapping-mobile. By the time I'd found him (he was next door at Janet's, *shnorring* cookies) and made sure that he understood that if he EVER disappeared again without telling me where he was going I would have to send him back to the orphanage, it was time to feed all three of them, give them their baths, and put them in their bunny suits. In the meantime, the glutinous cabbage was giving off such a pungent and yummy odor that who could tell that the chicken was being zapped by cancer-inducing, oven-cleaning rays?

Here's the chicken-and-artichoke recipe: Soak clay cooker. Place minced garlic, chopped-up onions, mushrooms, and whatever else might taste good (like carrots or apples) in the bottom of the cooker. Coat pieces of chicken with a flour-and-paprika mixture. Place chicken and canned artichoke hearts in cooker. Pour in some chicken broth and some sherry or wine. Place in cold oven. Then set oven at 425 degrees. Cook until done, about, in my case, never.

"Fuck," I said when I discovered my mistake. Then, seeing as I may have caused a slight ripple of embarrassment to my guests, I said: "I don't mean that literally." This, of course, made things worse, and I went around the rest of the evening wondering if I had said, "I don't mean that literally," or "I don't mean that clitorally." What *had* my boyfriend and I talked about so many years ago?

I did my best to clear up the confusion by explaining, calmly, that the chicken wasn't cooked. I had, however, managed to make the glutinous cabbage, the noodles, and the salad. (The trick to a good salad, besides fresh greens, is in the dressing. Here's a really yummy recipe that my friend Jane gave me: vegetable oil, regular old white vinegar, salt, pepper, Dijon-style mustard, and crumbled blue cheese. Fiddle with it until you get the proportions right.) My husband, God bless him, had brought good, fresh, crusty bread, from the upscale bread store down the street—the kind of store that also sells twenty-dollar jars of mushed-up imported black stuff in olive oil. "Come on into the dining room," I said. Then I said: "I mean: It's time for dinner. Why don't you enter the dining room?" Then I said: "Sorry." My husband, who usually has an office tan, was growing pink, and my boyfriend's wife was looking at me as if I had invited her over for dinner, only to forget to cook the chicken and then say a lot of stupid and incomprehensible things. And the whole time I was thinking about whether it would be ethical to ask *my* father if he could threaten to hold up partnership if my boyfriend should so much as breathe a word about me to my ex-friend?

We had plenty of wine, thank God. And in an effort to soothe over any discomfort, I decided to talk non-stop about anything that crossed my mind. Of course, my boyfriend's wife, who was about to have her second child, wasn't drinking, which was a shame, because she didn't seem to realize how completely hilarious all my little stories were, especially the one about how, years earlier, when my boyfriend called me this one time, I, in my nervousness, answered that I'd been waiting "breastlessly." Come to think of it, I mean, now that I'm thinking of it, my boyfriend didn't seem to think this story was very funny either. My husband was the color of the cabernet sauvignon. Total silence reigned.

Then we heard a loud thump followed by a piercing shriek from upstairs, where we had sent the two boys (my boyfriend's two-year-old in the care of Sam) to watch the *Sesame Street Hanukkah* video. We all ran up the stairs, where my boyfriend's son was lying on the floor with a bloody nose, and Sam was sitting on the sofa, with a little smirk on his face. "I had to teach him a lesson," he explained. Then he turned to my boyfriend's wife and asked: "Do you have a vagina?"

But the evening was not over yet, and I must report that my boyfriend and my boyfriend's wife remained calm and pleasant. We quieted the boys, checked on the twins, and went back to the dining room for dessert. Ah, yes. Strawberry sorbet with fresh strawberries. And these were really good, really fresh, really plump and juicy strawberries that I'd paid several thousand dollars for, at a new upscale gourmet natural food store near my house.

"Bottoms up," I said, lifting my glass and indicating the bowls of sorbet and strawberries before us. Then I realized that once again, I may have made an unintended sexual pun, and said: "Sweet and juicy, just the way I like it."

At the time, it seemed like hours elapsed before my

boyfriend and his family were gone. And while I can't deny that my husband and I got into a little tiff, and then stopped talking altogether, in retrospect, I'd say that the evening went fairly well. By the time my husband and I had cleaned up the dishes and gone upstairs, Sam had passed out on the sofa, and all we had to do was carry him, in his Aladdin pajamas, to bed. Rose and Jonathan were sleeping soundly. By the next afternoon, my husband and I were talking again, and I knew that no old boyfriend of mine could ever come between us.

SIX

Victual Reality

 BY THE TIME SPRING rolled around in earnest, my husband had all but forgotten about my boyfriend and had even stopped reminding me that, on the whole, it's better to smile and ask polite questions than to jabber on like a nit. By this time, too, he was so busy sending out his resumé and working on his shmoozing skills that he didn't much notice that his wife had actually started talking out loud to God, like Tevye in *Fiddler on the Roof.*

The truth is (and not that I want to get sentimentally stupid about it) that God and I were getting along really well. Even though I supplied most of the conversation, I felt that we'd established a good give-and-take. At least *He* listened, no matter how self-

absorbed or trivial I was. And unlike my therapist, He went ahead and gave me straightforward advice. For example, when I asked Him
why I had all these bizarre dreams about old boyfriends, He said: Big deal. And then when I asked Him
whether He thought my dreams indicated that my
own marriage was heading toward the skids, He went
and got Mrs. God, who said: Honey, you're still a little sleep deprived, and anyway, what makes you think
you're any different from the rest of Us? Then She said:
I think someone needs a dipey change. Naturally She
was right. Jonathan *was* giving off a rather pungent
odor—but my children were all so gorgeous, even the
big one, who still, on occasion, made tee-tee in his
bed, and my husband was so sweet, at least when he
wasn't pissed off at me, that I felt that I'd been singled
out for happiness. And I experienced this surge of
hope, of God in small moments, despite the fact that
the only thing my brother and sisters and I talked
about was whether Mom was going to last until sum-
mertime. It was, indeed, the season of Passover, with
its dual message of liberation and redemption—and its
wonderful ritual feast: the Seder.

But Mom kept getting worse and worse. She looked
like someone who had just been liberated from
Auschwitz, and, like many of them, she was also bald.
She'd long ago passed that point where she even *re-
membered* that chemotherapy was going to be "a snap."
Which meant, among other things, that she was too

busy trying to ward off the Angel of Death to cook a five-course dinner for twenty people. So my sisters and aunts and sister-in-law decided to make the Seder meal as best we could.

Even though Mom wasn't up to doing much cooking, I'd been boning up on my basic Judaism—having finally finished reading, among other texts, *The Jewish Way of Death and Mourning*—so I felt slightly better prepared for the ethical, historical, and religious aspects of the holiday than usual. Thus, when my sister Binky called to ask me to prepare a few side dishes as well as two ritual dishes (charoseth, made of chopped apples, walnuts, honey, and wine, a sweet dish that, ironically, symbolizes the mortar with which the Jewish slaves made bricks; and hard-boiled eggs—symbol of fertility), I said, "What about *Dad?* Isn't he going to do anything, or does he have better plans, such as flying all over the country buying up companies for his clients and then not talking to my old boyfriend about it even though they work together?" And my sister said: "You haven't quit therapy, have you, Jennifer?"

Actually, seeing as I was, by that point, on such a firm footing with the Big Guy, I was thinking about it. But that wasn't the point. The point was that Mom was sick, we were all in various stages of suspended animation, and *somebody* had to shoulder the blame. Why not Dad? He was the biggest. Plus he always took the blame for everything else that went wrong. Why not now? Made sense to me. After all, as my

second psychiatrist once said, Dad wouldn't
have had to pay for my therapy in the first place
if he hadn't been so weird to begin with—which
just goes to show you how simple it is to play the ra-
tionalization game.

As if she could read my mind, my sister then said:
"Don't you get tired of playing the role of perpetual angry adolescent?"

"No," I said.

Perhaps I was angry at Dad because, unaccountably,
he still seemed to think that Mom was going to be
okay. "Your mother will be better by summer," he kept
telling us. But her hair had fallen out in great clumps
one night when she was taking a shower; for days at a
stretch she was doubled over in pain; simple elimina-
tion was excruciating; and she'd lie on the sofa, in
agony, groaning. She became dehydrated and emaci-
ated; took antinausea drugs, sleeping pills, Prozac, and
Valium; her friends gave her little satchels of scented
soap and frilly pillows that said "Friends Forever," and
books on alternative medicines and how to get through
cancer by maintaining a macrobiotic diet. She moved
out of the bedroom she'd always shared with my father
and into one of the two twin beds in the room that had
once been Binky's. The house, which she'd always run
so efficiently, fell apart. Suddenly there were seams in
the walls and flaking paint, mold stains the size and
shape of Rorschach inkblots in the bathrooms, sagging
ceilings, layers of dust. My mother put up a kind of

shrine to her sister, Jane, in the bedroom that she'd taken over: a half-dozen photographs of the two of them, as children, stood on the dresser.

All this was on my mind as I spoke to my sister on the phone about which of us would make which dish for our family Seder at Mom and Dad's house. I was hoping that God would be with me, in my kitchen, when it was time to make the charoseth. My mother, I knew, didn't think God had much to do with cooking. She cooked for the sheer love of it—and of us. But I knew there was a bit of the divine in the best of her cooking. Even at Passover, when so many ingredients are off-limits, she was able to make food that tasted of all the richness and variance of life.

So I made the charoseth, and a salad, and some vegetables, and one sister made Grandma's Passover cake, and another sister made the matzoh ball soup, and my sister-in-law, who tends to do everything well, made the main course. Notice, here, that none of the men—not my husband, nor my brother, nor father, nor brother-in-law—cooked a damn thing. Even though all the women in the family, with the exception of me, are workaholic professionals with closets full of Ann Taylor suits.

Most of these recipes are pretty straightforward affairs, and as long as you don't coat your chicken in, say, bread crumbs, it will be kosher for Pesach. But the one thing that isn't so easy to make—I know, because I've never made it—is my mother's matzoh ball soup. This soup is so superior that even my husband, who always defends his own mother in the competition of the grandmothers, said as much. Specifically, he said: "This is by far and away the best matzoh ball soup I've ever tasted. Is there any chance whatsoever that you could ever learn to make it?"

I called Mom a few days before Passover began to get the recipe. She was eager to talk. This is what she said:

"First I go to the Giant and buy a ton of—what's that stuff called? You know, the beef with the bone in it? The bone marrow stuff. I make enough for a dozen people, so I always buy about eight bags or so. It's mostly meat, like a steak, but with this round bone in the middle of it. Then I buy one chunk of beef—something that's going to shred, like a shoulder or a brisket. Separate the meat, and put half in one big pot and half in another big pot. Cover it all with water in your two big pots, up to the top. Bring the meat to a boil on high heat. You'll see the fat float up. *Take the fat off immediately.* That's important. That's what makes the soup clear. The white yucky stuff comes off first thing. But the brownish-whitish gook is harder to take off; it takes a few minutes. When you've got all the fat off, turn the heat down to low. Then put in some onions, some bay leaf, a turnip if you have one, a little salt and pepper, and *then* put the lid on almost tight but not completely tight. Then you'll need to cook the whole shebang for three or four hours, so it condenses but it doesn't boil over. After about four hours, I let the soup cool. Then I put it in the fridge overnight. In the morning I take all the meat out and all the everything else out too—onions, et cetera. Then I cut up the meat and put a little bit back in. Then the clearish soup goes back on the stove. If there's any fat left over, get rid of it. Then you doctor it up."

Mom stopped to rest. Then she said: "This is really why my soup is better than Grandma Helene's, only don't tell her that I said so. Not that she can hear anything anyhow, poor thing. Deaf as a post, blind as a bat."

She paused again, then said: "Listen, while I've got you on the phone, would you please start thinking about what jewelry of mine you want. I'm going to give my ruby ring to Rose.

"Wait a second, I think I'm going to be sick. No, it's okay now. Are you listening, Jennifer? Okay, at this point, once the soup is clear, I usually add some beef bouillon, then a can of tomatoes and a little sugar, and maybe a little ketchup, and a little worcestershire, and some more salt and pepper. I put just a *little* bit of the meat back in. The rest is for the dogs. The dogs eat well at Pesach.

"You know, to tell you the truth, I don't think I'm going to be around for too many more Passovers, and I want all you children to know that I don't want to prolong my life at the end. Did I tell you that I've been reading about how people with terminal cancer kill themselves? Usually they do it with sleeping pills, but it has to be the exact right amount of pills and booze, or you could vomit it all up and survive. It has to be done just right, you understand?"

I didn't answer.

"I don't want your father's second wife to get my mother's furniture, okay? Are you listening, Jennifer?

"Fine then. For the matzoh balls, these are the proportions. Of course I multiply it all by about twenty. Ready? Two matzohs, two tablespoons chicken fat, two eggs, a chopped onion, chopped parsley, one cup of matzoh meal, salt, pepper, ginger, nutmeg. First you soak the matzohs in cold water. Squeeze them dry. Heat the fat in a skillet, add onion, fry to golden brown. Add soaked matzohs until the whole mixture comes up off the skillet without any leftover gunk. Add the seasonings, slightly beaten eggs, and matzoh meal. The whole mess is still in the pan. Let it stand on the stove for several hours with no heat, and it will swell up. Then shape it into balls. I usually do this a few days ahead, and then freeze the balls in wax paper in the freezer.

"Were you serious when you said that your husband was trying to get a *teaching* job? You mean he'd leave the firm? But, Jennifer, you don't mean to tell me that you'd leave Washington? You can't be serious. But if he gets a teaching job, you could end up *anywhere*. I mean, you could end up in some dreadful place like, I don't know, Louisiana or someplace else where it's hot all the time, and you know how you hate the heat.

Don't forget that Aunt Claire followed *her* husband to New Orleans all those years ago, and she *still* gripes about how far away it is. Have you ever been to New Orleans in the summer? It's so hot you can't even breathe.

"Okay, let's not talk about it, then. Forget I said anything. Just don't go too far away. Okay, we *won't* discuss it anymore. My lips are sealed. Why are you so defensive? Did I tell you that Binky is coming down from New York a couple of days early so she can be my personal shopper? I need a new dress. Nothing fits anymore. Do you think I ought to buy something now for my funeral? Or is that too morbid?"

Amazingly, Mom managed to get herself up and dressed for the Seder. She sat in her customary place at the end of the table, with a small, forced smile on her face. She was wearing the wig she'd had made before the chemotherapy treatments began. She picked at her food and watched the grandchildren. We tried to be cheerful—to sing the songs and make the usual corny jokes—but it was hard to really get into the spirit of the holiday and to ask, for example, "Why is this night different from all other nights?" when Mom could barely eat a single bite of chicken. At his end of the table, Dad looked drawn, and for the first time in my life, I looked at him and realized that he was getting old. His beautiful silver hair was thin on top; his eyes were hooded; his face was lined. My parents had recently celebrated their fortieth wedding anniversary, and it was hard to imagine him without Mom. For that matter, I couldn't begin to accept that Mom herself could vanish from our midst.

Sometime before dessert, she went back to bed. Her two eldest grandchildren, Sam and his cousin Sarah, followed her into her room and sat on the floor next to her bed, begging her for stories.

"Mom," Sam asked after dinner, as we drove back to our own house, "is Grammy going to die?"

"Go to sleep," I told him.

I had a stomachache. I've been plagued by stomachaches all my life, so I wasn't particularly alarmed about this one, which, if it wasn't a tumor, was probably merely proof that I'd had too many pieces of Grandma's Passover cake. As a child, I always got a stomachache during Seder, which we celebrated at my grandparents' in Baltimore. This is what would happen: For days and days before Seder, I'd worry about how stupid I'd look when it was my turn to read from the Haggadah, because I'd be sure to mispronounce some long word, like *embryonic,* or *Abrahamitic,* or even, if I were particularly nervous, *rabbinic.* The minute we arrived at Grandma and Pop's, I'd know for sure that I was in serious doo-doo, because someone, usually my grandfather, would ask me how school was. School? You mean that place where I was pulling in a straight C-minus average? Then we'd be called to the table, and I'd sit there, sweating through my Pesach dress, as my grandfather read the Hebrew prayers so fast that he ran out of

breath (never, *ever* skipping a single one, meaning
that we kids had to sit through the recitation of
countless Talmudic debates about the particular
meaning, for example, of the phrase, "one day"), the
grown-ups sang, and the cousins, when asked, would
mention that they'd just won a few dozen National
Merit scholarships. At some point, usually around the
time that Grandma rang her little bell to signal to the
"girls" in the kitchen that it was time to serve the spiced
peaches, I would slink off to my grandparents' bedroom to work on an incipient ulcer.

Finally, when I was eleven, and a student in Mrs.
Kohn's sixth-grade class at the Potomac School in
McLean, Virginia, I developed an ulcer in earnest. My
classmates were from a different world, possessed of a
kind of Waspy savoir faire coupled with athletic ability
that I pretended to disdain and secretly, and passionately, longed to replicate. Though at school I'd been
unable to distinguish myself in any way, my ulcer
briefly gave me status. I brought my bottle of Maalox
with me to school in my bookbag, and at lunch, when
all the other kids were eating the lumpy, gray hunks of
flesh that the school dietitian described as "sloppy
joes," or the pink goop swimming in white slime which
every kid knew was a dead ringer for fresh vomit but
was called "chipped beef," I was allowed to go to the
teacher's "buffet" and heap onto my plate as many
cubes of green Jello and as much cottage cheese as I
wanted. I don't know why I got an ulcer. I was a dark,

unhappy, sullen child with a lot of curly hair and a neurotic fear of Nazis, and I loved my mother with a passion that I've never felt for any other person, and every now and then my stomach hurt so bad that I couldn't walk.

Old joke:

Q: What do you call a Jewish after-dinner mint?

A: Tums.

The really bad part about my stomachaches was that I frequently missed out on the best part of the Seder meal, namely, dessert. For years and years, my grandmother, Helene Moses, made the cake herself. Then she got too old, and she gave the recipe to my mother. Here it is:

Grandma's Passover Cake (The Best in Baltimore and, Probably, the World)

12 eggs, separated

2 cups sugar

1½ teaspoons cinnamon

¼ teaspoon ground cloves

⅓ cup sweet kosher wine

1½ cup matzoh flour

1 cup chopped, blanched almonds

Preheat oven to 325 degrees. Beat egg yolks and sugar until very light. Add spices, wine, matzoh flour, and almonds. Fold in stiffly beaten egg whites. Bake in large, ungreased tube pan for about 1 hour. Frost cake.

To ice the cake you need:

1 cup granulated sugar
½ cup water
2 egg whites
½ teaspoon sweet kosher wine

Boil sugar and water over low heat until syrup spins a thread. Pour very slowly into stiff egg whites, and beat until smooth and stiff enough to spread. Add sweet wine.

By the time we got home, the children had all fallen asleep, and my stomach was feeling better. We carried them inside and put them into their beds and stood over them, watching them dream. They were brand new and perfect. They were God's gift to us.

Much later, as I drifted off to sleep, I saw all the women in my family—all the women who had given me life. There was my mother's mother, Jennie, roasting a chicken; there was Grandma Helene, fussing over her Passover cakes; and there was my mother, her hands coated with cake batter, her heart swollen with love.

SEVEN

Mastering the Art of French Kissing

THIS IS PERHAPS an unfeminist thing to admit, but ever since I was old enough to play dress-up, I desperately wanted to get married. I both desperately wanted to get married and was desperately afraid that I never would. Because, to summarize, who the hell would want to marry *me?* And then, if I ever did meet someone who both wanted to marry me and I wanted to marry back, how could I continue being a budding literary genius who lived on the top floor of a six-floor walk-up in the East Village with views of drag queens parading in Tompkins Square Park? And what about my love life? How could I go around complaining to my girlfriends about my unhealthy and obsessive love life if I were happily married? It seemed like a lot to give up. On the other hand, my mother had been dragging me with her to look at china for such a long time that I couldn't remember a time when I didn't want to replicate my mother's fantasy for me and find ordinary, simple happiness. Plus, I figured that, if I was going to get married, I may as well do it while I was still young enough to have kids.

But I couldn't figure out how it was *done*. As far as I could tell, there were only two kinds of men in the world: really cool good-looking powerful men—who, as a bonus, made me feel like shit—and limp-wristed wimpy nerds from the Midwest. Then I met my husband, and *voilà!* Four years and tons of therapy later, Grandma Lola told him that he better marry me or else. The next thing I know, I'm shopping for dishes.

For a full year before my wedding day, I spent hours, daily, mooning over those fat glossy bridal magazines that tell you how to do everything but give your husband a blow job. I'd sit there, in the windowless brown cubby I occupied (I had by that time left my job as a typist at *Mademoiselle,* and was now working at Reader's Digest books), gazing at the beautiful photographs of gorgeous brides, when I was supposed to be editing copy on, for example, how to make your own sandpaper. ("Take two or three pieces of flexible cardboard. Coat with rubber cement. Lay rubber-cement-coated cardboard face down in sandbox. *Voilà!* Sandpaper.") I couldn't focus. I'd flip through the pages of the bridal magazines, fantasizing about the moment when I would enter the sacred covenant of matrimony and . . .

And *what?* Finally learn how to "French kiss" properly—the art of which had eluded me ever since my friend Barbara had told me about this disgusting practice in the fifth grade? Or, better yet, learn how to swallow without thinking about milk of magnesia?

It didn't matter. What mattered was that Mom had been waiting a long, long time for one of her girls *finally* to get with it and get married already, because, after all, *all* her friends' daughters were already married to successful cardiologists who were extremely nice to their mothers-in-law. What I'm trying to convey is that by the time I announced my engagement, Mom, who'd been browsing bridal registries for more than three decades, was prepared. My wedding was a full Cinderella: the long white dress, the *chuppah,* the string quartet. Even the dogs were dressed up, in ribbons and bow ties. Mom was ecstatic. Dad was happy too, I guess. Actually, I don't think he was fully prepared to see me walk off with another man—and just because he actually grabbed me away from my husband mere minutes after my husband and I had exchanged our *"Ha-rei aht me-ku-deshet li be-ta-ba'aht zoh, ke-daht Moshe ve-Yisra'el"*'s and insisted that *he,* rather than my husband, walk me into the large, striped canvas tent where the reception was being held—what of it? It didn't mean that he wasn't secretly thrilled that I was about to have my honeymoon night. How would I know, anyhow? The man doesn't talk. And, anyhow, the point is: I got married, and every year, sometime in spring, my mother calls me to remind me that my anniversary is coming up.

"Jennifer," Mom said in mid-May. "This is your mother."

"Hi, Mom."

"Wasn't that a beautiful wedding?"

"What?"

"I was looking through your wedding album today."

"Are you feeling any better?"

"What do you want for your anniversary? Would you like my good china?"

An hour or so after I'd swallowed a half-bottle of cherry-flavored Maalox, I saw that Mom had a point. The anniversary of our marriage was right around the corner, and it was an occasion to celebrate with a romantic dinner. Thus it was that I made dinner reservations. Then I started calling around for a baby-sitter. I called my mother's former cleaning lady, my mother's former cleaning lady's daughter, my brother's regular sitter, my sister-in-law's regular sitter and her daughter, the teenage sons and daughters of several friends and neighbors, my next-door-neighbor's nanny's best friend who was a nanny for a *Washington Post* writer who was rarely home, and a half-dozen people randomly selected from the Washington, D.C., phone book. Everyone I called said, "Forget about it, lady, and while I've got you on the phone, may I just say that your college roommate Susan was right when she told you it was time to start coloring your hair?" It was in this manner that I was forced to bite the bullet and make my own damn romantic dinner.

My mind started filling with images of fabulously yummy things, like roasted peppers, and gleaming artichokes stuffed with, say, a little foie gras or aioli, all artfully arranged on vintage platters and displayed on a table set with big bowls of red roses. All I needed was a chef and a food stylist—or perhaps just my neighbor, Janet—and I'd be all set.

No, not really. Because summer (especially early summer, before global warming turns Washington into the gaseous, soupy swamp that it later becomes, particularly if you're within earshot of a politician) makes meal planning easy. Warm days, cool nights, dogwood trees blossoming, children playing street soccer in front of your house. It's like living inside a Norman Rockwell painting. Thus it was that I'd gone ahead and planted my vegetable garden, where even now, basil, red and green bell peppers, and a variety of tomatoes were pushing up out of the ground. Actually, planting your own vegetable garden was fairly de rigeur in my neighborhood, even if you didn't take care of it because you were too busy flying to Des Moines to litigate a case involving faulty ceiling-fan parts. But I was serious about my vegetable garden. My mother always had a vegetable garden, and every fall, she and one of my sisters would spend days making chow-chow and jams and soups. My own garden wasn't very impressive, but I loved it. It made me feel so earth-mothery.

Actually, that's a lie. Mainly it made me feel dirty and sweaty. But it also made me feel that maybe that ache in my side wasn't a budding tumor but merely a cramp. So it was in a mood of creativity that I sat down at the kitchen table and started looking in earnest for festive summer recipes.

(While I'm on the subject, let me offer my favorite of all my favorite really easy summer dishes that anyone, even my husband, can make: spaghetti with chopped tomatoes, olive oil, and basil. What you do is: Chop up some fresh tomatoes, shred up some fresh basil, mix them together in a bowl with olive oil, salt, and pepper, and a little chopped garlic and shredded parmesan cheese. Pour the mixture over cooked spaghetti. *Voilà!* Dinner.)

For our romantic dinner, I decided to make: pizza covered with fresh pesto and tomatoes, followed by grilled tuna steaks on a bed of salsa, accompanied by green salad and bread. Good, fresh, crusty bread. All this would be washed down by white wine. Finally, *le dessert.* Four years of courtship. Five years of marriage. Three healthy children. The best basil patch on the block. We had a lot to celebrate, after all. Double double-chocolate mousse cake? Strawberry truffle torte? Creme caramel? I decided on something more realistic, but equally delicious and celebratory: chocolate fudge brownies, straight from the box.

The idea, naturally enough, was that I was going to prepare all this well in advance of the romantic dinner itself, and I was going to have flowers on the table, and wine, and, on our new CD player that Mom had given us for Hanukkah even though she was too sick to go shopping, I'd be playing the kind of touchy-feely soft-rock music that's always playing on the soundtrack when the beautiful heroine and handsome hero in the movie finally do it. *Plus* I was going to be freshly showered, and wearing something so pretty that my husband was going to think that I was actually Andie McDowell. And rather than talk about cancer, I was going to say things to my husband like:

> *Those set our hairs, but these our flesh upright*
> *License my roving hands, and let them go,*
> *Before, behind, between, above, below.*
>   (JOHN DONNE)

Speaking of roving hands, I'd made all this stuff before, and all of it's easy. The pizza covered with pesto, for instance. You can be serious and make your own pizza dough, which I've been told isn't hard, especially if you have a bread machine, or you can get real and buy a Boboli pizza shell (or a Boboli knock-off) at your supermarket. Then you just pluck your fresh-grown basil from your requisite yuppie basil patch and throw it together with your olive oil, garlic, Parmesan, walnuts or pine nuts, and even a little melted butter, if you're feeling sinful, and glomp it together in your food processor. (My own food processor was a gift from Grandma Lola. At first it scared me. I mean, all those metal *parts*. But now, if I do say so myself, I'm quite capable of using it without chopping off any of my fingers.)

I guess by now everyone knows that pesto (literally, "it's an acquired taste") is a snap to make. So you make your pesto, and slather it atop your pizza shell. Then you slice up some fresh tomatoes and layer them on top and bake at 450 degrees for ten or twelve minutes . . . seriously delish, and what could be easier? Only I forgot to buy the walnuts, and my neighbors were all out litigating, so I couldn't borrow from them. Even worse, Janet—who might have actually made dinner for me had she been available—wasn't home. Almonds? Why not? Because that's the neat thing about cooking. You don't have to go by the book, and the best cooks, as well as the most harried ones, almost never do.

This is what my husband said when he bit into my homemade pesto-and-tomato pizza:

"Interesting."

And I said:

"What's your problem?"

Then Sam came down the stairs carrying Willy-Billy, his stuffed tyrannosaurus rex, and said:

"There are bees in my room."

So I went upstairs, to get the bees out of his room, only guess what? There were no bees. I turned on the light. Still no bees. Sam's eyes were wide open. He was screaming: "Bees! Bees! Get them off of me!" I sat next to him on the bed, holding his hand, while I explained to him, for the fifth or sixth time that week, about his imagination. (As if I'm one to talk. For several months after I saw *The Silence of the Lambs,* I couldn't go to sleep until I'd checked under all the beds and in all the closets to make sure that Hannibal the Cannibal wasn't in my house.) "Look at me, Sam," I said. And all of a sudden Sam came out of his trance and fell asleep. By the time I returned to dinner, my husband was engrossed in an article called "Regulatory Practices in the Pharmaceutical Industry," and the pesto on the pesto-and-tomato pizza had congealed.

An elaboration here, while I'm on the subject of things congealed, on my premarital versus my postmarital love life: One of the givens of getting married is that you're no longer allowed to flirt, except in the safe, dull, cutesy way of a nurse in an old-age home. Not being allowed to flirt was for some time a real problem for me, as it is for many other neurotic people. If you have a very, very shaky ego—and generally believe that everyone hates you because of all your neurotic shit about how corrupt you are inside because, just to cite one example, when you were a child you used to dance naked in front of the mirror, imagining yourself as Josephine Baker, which in itself set up more crazy stuff about why the SS was after you which was why your parents preferred your much smarter older sister who by the way at least had breasts big enough to fill out a training bra—getting boys to fall in love with you gives you this sort of temporary feeling of power. But *then* what happens is that suddenly you have this very serious boyfriend who gives you nice presents and he wants to introduce you to his parents, only you don't even like him. Which at least lends a little drama to your life. Compare this with my postmarital love life, wherein I shared a bed every night with my true love, only for months after our twins were born, we were too tired to so much as think about doing the thang-thing.

"Dearest?" I said.

"Let me just finish this paragraph," he said.

"Hungry?" I said.

"Why did I ever decide to become a lawyer?" he said.

I got up to get the entrée. Everything was so pretty. We were sitting on our screened-in porch; I'd set the table with flowers and candles; we were surrounded by the lush, viney things that grew in our backyard; and the sky was filled with the sounds of crickets. After all, it was our *romantic* dinner—the kind of dinner that longish-married couples plan in order to get all goopy about each other and fall into bed and make passionate love and feel, once again, that they aren't married. Or at least not to each other.

And seeing that I'm once again on the subject of sex, let me just say this: Never, ever, not even in a million years, would I greet my husband at the doorway wearing nothing but a pair of black silk stockings and a whip, even if such a get-up were immediately to lead to a bout of French kissing followed by fabulous five-alarm sex. I mention this because right around the time of my anniversary, I had an assignment to write an article about how your sex life can take a nosedive after you have kids, only I'm not going to name the woman's magazine that wanted me to write the article, because that would be unprofessional. Okay. Let's call the magazine *"Bluebook."* *"Bluebook"* asked me to write an article called "The Diary of a Once-Hot Housewife"— their title, not mine. Now what I want to know is: How did *"Bluebook"* know that I *might* fall under that particular rubric? Had they been spying on me? Perhaps they had been tracking me over the years, and even now had placed a hidden video camera over my bed? It was an incredibly humiliating assignment. But because I was so desperate for money and attention, I'd agreed to prostitute myself and write the damn thing. What the editors of *"Bluebook"* wanted me to do was to experiment with different techniques designed to turn my husband and myself into horny fifteen-year-olds in the backseat of a Chevy, and then write about it. The idea was that *"Bluebook's"* readers were looking for reassurance that (a) it's not unusual for most women—with the exception of those women, like the editors of *"Bluebook,"* who have nicer clothes than the rest of us—to feel like sexless frumps after a few years of matrimony and (b) not wearing underwear under your very short miniskirt when you go out to a fancy French restaurant may well lead to really really hot sex with the waiter. Seriously, what *"Bluebook"* wanted me to do was try to come up with ways that *"Bluebook's"* readers might rev up what had become their less than passionate sex lives in the wake of producing children, who, as everyone knows, have a tendency to start screaming about bees the very minute your husband turns to you to say: "How about it, my sweet ripe peach?"

But even though I really wanted the three thousand five hundred dollars that they were going to pay me for this piece of junk, not to mention the attention I was going to get when Oprah herself invited me onto her show to discuss it, in the end I just couldn't write it the way they wanted me to. The problem was, I kept coming back to this idea that if your sex life goes down the toilet after you have kids, wearing a negligee or telling your husband to call you "kinky kitten" or even watching pornographic movies isn't going to do anything but make you feel stupid, unless, of course, you're into sex play to begin with, thank you very much but I already enjoy being tied to the bed while my husband rips my clothes off me with a steak knife. *"Bluebook"* ended up

"killing" what I'd written, and the worst part
about it—other than the fact that I didn't get the
dough—was that my pathetic little ego, always
grasping for admiration, just shriveled up and died.
And in the very next issue of *"Bluebook,"* which I read
while waiting at the three-mile-long supermarket
check-out line, there was an article called "Ten Ways to
Make Your Husband Want You" (or something along
those lines) that I memorized, and then told my shrink
about. And do you know what she said? She said:
"What are your thoughts?"

Anyone can make grilled tuna steaks. You can mari-
nate them first, or just let them go naked onto the
flame. (I used my mother-in-law's marinade: chopped
garlic, white vinegar, a little olive oil, a little sesame oil,
a little Dijon mustard, a whole bunch of ground ginger,
and soy sauce.) If you have an old-fashioned grill, like
we have, you have to remember to light the fire—I
mean, charcoal. But even if you forget to light the grill,
you can still make really good fish in your regular old
oven, which is what I did. And I mean these were fresh,
thick, juicy steaks that I'd paid a fortune for at our local
upscale yuppie gourmet natural foods store. So into the
oven with you, you old tuna steaks!

The salsa: There are a lot of good salsa recipes and,
believe me, fresh salsa—the kind made by chopping
up a lot of ripe tomatoes with plenty of fresh cilantro
and parsley, and lemon and lime juice and a little
Tabasco and salt and pepper—is not only easy to

make, but absolutely not to be compared with the kind of salsa you stick your chips in at badly lit bars. The difference is in the tomatoes. Because what can compare with a good fresh tomato, the kind found at roadside stands if you happen to live in California? I made the salsa, but then somehow managed to drop it on the floor. The bowl just sort of jumped out of my hands. It was really weird. But I did have a bottle of Chi-Chi's famous salsa in my kitchen cupboard, so we were golden.

Plus I had a loaf of good, fresh, crusty bread. With bread, you shouldn't take chances. That's why I didn't bake it myself.

I didn't want to take a chance with the salad either. These days you can get "mesclun," also known as expensive salad mix, just about anywhere. And here's an elegantly easy dressing: red wine vinegar, olive oil, Dijon mustard, pinch of chopped garlic, and sugar. Fiddle with the proportions until you get them right.

Why, you may ask, if I was actually going ahead and planning this dinner à deux in order to end up falling into bed and making love until God Himself had to take a peek (though the last time I'd talked to Him, He promised He wouldn't), did I forget so many ingredients? It's a long story, but basically what happened was this: First, Jonathan got the croup, and we were afraid his throat would swell up and he'd die, and I spent several nights sleeping on the floor of the twins' room developing a bad back. Then Rose came down with an ear infection, and her pediatrician put her on an antibiotic, only Rose was allergic to the antibiotic, and her entire body swelled up to twice its normal size and she was covered with these enormous red welts. Then the imaginary bees started visiting Sam's room at night—and in the middle of all this Mom called me and said, "Can you take me to the emergency room? Dad's out of town, and I think I'm dying." We were becoming dysfunctional. We were seriously thinking about becoming born-again Christians.

"*Voilà!*" I said to my husband. "*L'entrée.*" I then put his plate before him: the grilled, except that it was baked, tuna on a bed of salsa. The *salade de fancée lettuce.* The crusty bed, I mean bread. I reached over and poured the wine. My husband lifted his fork, took a bite.

"This tastes like Chi-Chi's," he said.

And I said:

"Go ahead, rain on my parade."

And from upstairs we heard a thud, and then a wail, and when we went to investigate, we found that Jonathan had managed to pull himself up and over the crib railing and had landed on the floor. By the time we had quieted him down and had our pediatrician paged and had talked to her and seen with our own eyes that Jonathan was still breathing, the tuna steaks had turned green. But I'd like to report that the salad and the bread were both quite delicious, and anyhow, once you've had three, four glasses of chardonnay in you, who cares about dead green tuna steaks?

Also, we still had dessert coming our way. Even the most harried cook can't mess up Duncan Hines chocolate brownies, unless you overcook them. I don't honestly know why anyone bothers with making brownies from scratch anymore. My mother made brownies from scratch, and I used to, too. The mixes are almost as good, only, of course, they've got all these weird ingredients in them that could gunk up your yin-and-yang.

For Mom's recipe, you will need:

½ cup butter
1 cup sugar
2 eggs
2 ounces baker's chocolate, melted
½ cup flour
½ teaspoon vanilla

Cream the butter and sugar in a mixer. Add the eggs, one at a time. Add the other stuff. Pour into a greased eight-by-eight-inch pan. Bake in a preheated 350-degree oven for fifteen to twenty minutes.

As we sat in the soft, mellow glow of candlelight, eating our Duncan Hines brownies, we thought about our years together, the children we'd been blessed with, and the dirty dishes moldering away in the sink.

And my husband said:

"Yummy good dinner, Jen."

And I said:

"Happy anniversary."

Our children were sleeping. The night was filled with stars.

EIGHT

Let Them Eat
Ice Cream Cake

 NOW THAT IT WAS SUMMER, I couldn't help but notice that Sam was out of school. This was problematic, because when little boys are home, they spend most of their waking hours either utzing their mothers to drive them to the shopping mall to see the latest Disney movie, or conducting scientific experiments involving toothpaste, mud, beer, and your best china. I wasn't getting much done. Even though I was doing a million things at once, not one of them consisted of having a complete thought or uttering a single complete sentence, not to mention completing a best-selling literary novel that would at last land me on the talk-show circuit. So when, in late June, my friend Melanie wrote to let me know, among

other things, that her second book would soon
be published, I had such an acute attack of envy
that my hair actually turned green.

As if on cue, Grandma Lola called mere minutes after I'd burned Melanie's letter and asked, "What's up?"
"My friend Melanie is about to publish her second
book and I have so many rejection slips I could wallpaper my entire house with them," I answered. Now
the thing about Grandma Lola is: She's always been on
my side. Whenever I've been really down, she's picked
me up. She listened as I explained how I was so eaten
up with envy that I now resembled the Wicked Witch
from *The Wizard of Oz,* only not as fashionably attired—and not only that, but even if I ever did write
something halfway decent, my mother probably
wouldn't be around to see it, so what was the point?
And when I was done, Grandma Lola said: "I know it's
a long road, but you're getting there, and Jennifer, after all, there's a birthday candle at the end of the tun-
nel." "Huh?" I said. It was at this point that she
reminded me that my children's birthdays were right
around the corner, in August, which was just six or
seven weeks away, and moreover, of course she'd love
to come to their parties, and it was no trouble that
Sam's birthday was on the first of the month and the
twins' two weeks later, because she'd come for Sam's
and just stay, because, after all, what kind of life is it if
you don't stop and smell the coffee? "And as long as
we're on the subject," she said, "could you please tell

me what the children want for their birthday presents?"

"I don't know," I said.

"Well, would you please think about it?"

"Uh."

"What are you doing for their parties?"

"I don't know."

"Are you aware that you *have* children?" she said.

Part of the problem was that in our neck of the woods, birthday parties tended toward excess. An example is the birthday party where the four-year-old birthday girl's mother hired a fleet of stretch limousines to take the children to the zoo. Or the one Sam went to where the five-year-old's friends went to a real, live rifle range, where they got to practice their shooting skills. Personally I've always preferred old-fashioned at-home parties, but they too are less than ideal. The problem with at-home birthday parties is that they're at home. Meaning that, just for starters, the guests will leave pee-pee on every toilet seat.

What I'm trying to convey is that I'd never figured out how to give a birthday party that would both be fun for the kids and easy on our furniture, our bank account, and my nerves, which were due for a tune-up, or possibly a replacement. Already we'd accompanied Sam to so many extravagant affairs that the very concept of children's birthday parties had begun to—not to put too fine a point on it—nauseate me. The bottom line was that I wanted to ignore the whole concept.

Couldn't we just give each of them their own little set of Proust and be done with it?

Of course, when we first got into the kid
racket, my husband and I didn't even know from birthday parties. We were young; Sam smelled like cookie
dough; his skin felt like butter; even his wee-wee was
cute. We'd never even heard of Chuck-E-Cheese, let
alone been assaulted by a birthday party there. But little by little, without even knowing it, we'd been drawn
into this revolting orgy of ice cream and cake that goes
under the rubric of "children's birthday parties." It had
all started out so innocently, too, the year that Sam
turned one, and my husband and I—reasoning that a
one-year-old child wouldn't notice whether he had a
birthday party—took a little vacation, leaving him
with my parents.

"We had a little celebration here, nothing much,"
Mom said when we called on Sam's birthday to see how
things were going. "Wait a minute, I'm going to put
him on the phone. Here he is."

"Sam?" I said.

"Cake," he said.

"It's Mommy, Sam."

"Balloons. Ice cream. Candles."

"We'll be home soon, sweetheart."

"Bring present?"

But now my mother was so sick that she couldn't
even compete with me, and as Grandma Lola had
pointed out, it would soon be August—the month

when all three of my children were born. After I got off the phone, I looked up and saw that Sam was on the brink of five. I also noticed that he had mysteriously morphed into a person whose greatest interest in life, in addition to tracking mud up the stairs, was collecting dead insects. He was, moreover, *big*, with these long, skinny arms and long, skinny legs. He was sophisticated enough to know how to interrupt me the very minute I tried to pay bills or have an adult conversation, ask probing, difficult questions about sex and death, and deconstruct modernist poetry, which he said was (quoting Harry S. Truman) largely "hooey." His top dresser drawer was filled with Spider Man underwear and mismatched filthy socks—and where had all this *come* from? He was no longer a cuddly dumpling. My feelings for him had changed. I could not for the life of me understand why I loved him so much.

Moreover, the twins were about to turn *one*. They'd officially crossed the threshold from infancy to toddlerhood. One day I caught them studying the Dr. Spock entries on "discovering autonomy." The *next* day I found them toddling out the front door and into the street. I could no longer keep up with them. They were mobile. And their birthdays were coming up. The corollary being that, before I knew it, they'd be too old to kiss on their tummies. In fact, if the birthday trend continued as I prayed it would, in no time flat my children wouldn't even want to hang out with their geeky parents at all, and would no doubt add insult to injury by telling all their friends how embarrassing it was to be related to us, as I myself had done. Birthday party? Why the hell should I give any one of the little ingrates a birthday party?

Okay, I'll admit it. I'm somewhat ambivalent about the subject. I'm easily sucked into the birthday-party-memory vortex, where I start crying. Of course, children's birthday parties *were* different in the olden days. In the olden days, you wake in the morning to discover that it's your birthday. Your mother makes you your favorite cake. She makes it herself, in the mixer, with eggs and milk and sugar. You get to lick the spoon. Later, your friends come over, wearing pretty party dresses in orange and pink and pale pale blue. They have ribbons in their hair. It's high summer—blue sky, long grass, the buzz of crickets, the hum of birds in the trees. In the playroom, you play Pin the Tail on the Donkey. In the backyard, you have a Treasure Hunt. Later everyone sings "Happy Birthday to You," and you have ice cream and cake. Your mother kisses you. She's young: with her pretty short black hair, in her summer shifts, her strong legs flashing: And how desperately you want to be like her, always so cheerful, so pretty—teaching you to do the Charleston in the living room, your legs working crazily, your arms swinging like batons. And how sad she is, too, how overwhelmed by what you've done to her, you and your sisters and brother. Once she was a girl in a cashmere sweater and saddle shoes, doing crazy cartwheels across a football field. Now she is the woman who is left behind in the house on the hill. Her beloved father, Clarence, dead from cancer: She gazes at his portrait in the living room, her eyes misting with tears. He loved me so much, Jennifer. He loved *all* of us. But now he's dead: dead before you were born; dead when you were just a cluster of cells in your mother's body. Maybe you killed him, after all; maybe he died to make room for you. How odd it all is. But you've seen the marks across her stomach, the rubbery creases where the doctors cut her open. Who were you then? And who was *she?* Did she cry when her father died? He's dead: dead dead dead. You can't remember a time when she didn't talk of him with such longing that the air around her seemed to weep. Is your grandfather in heaven? Is your own father going to die too? What if he had a heart attack? How could you—how could any of you—go on without him? What's wrong with you? It's your birthday, your party. "Make a wish," your mother says. You close your eyes—and wish and wish and wish and wish that you could be pretty, pretty like Mommy. And there's Daddy—he's standing next to Mommy, humming the Happy Birthday song. Later he leans over you and gently touches the top of your head with his fingertips. You open your presents—a book, a doll, a mood ring. Afterward, you get a stomachache.

"Mom," Sam said one afternoon while I was in my home "office" trying to balance my checkbook after the bank sent me a nice letter telling me that I had overdrawn my account even though I could have SWORN that I had at least four hundred and twenty-seven dollars and eighty-two cents in it.

"Go away," I said.

"But Mom, it's *important*," he insisted.

"Is the house burning down?"

"No."

"Are the twins playing in the street?"

"No."

"Are there bees in your room?"

"No."

"Then it can wait."

"Mom, do you have PMS or something?" Sam said.

"No."

"Have you planned my BIRTHDAY PARTY?"

"Uh," I said.

"Because this year, for my birthday party, I want to go to that place, I forget the name of it, that place where Jeffrey had his birthday, you know, in the mall, the Playzone or something, and we'll play on the tubes and then go into the birthday room and have a Ninja birthday party. I want a real black belt karate white Ninja to teach us his best karate moves. I want pizza, and Coke, and two cakes—one chocolate, the other vanilla. And what I want is, I want Nintendo, a whole book of baseball cards, lots of comic books, two dozen Supersoakers, and twenty-five dollars just to spend on whatever I want, and don't forget my own TV with remote control so I can play Nintendo in my room."

I was about to burst into tears from the sheer frustration of trying to balance my checking account when I still hadn't mastered basic subtraction skills, and had to check and recheck on my fingers even though I had a perfectly good working pocket calculator—not to mention that Sam smelled vaguely of dog-doo— when the phone rang. It was Binky. "I have bad news," she said. I braced myself to hear that Mom's cancer had spread. But what she told me was even worse. She was calling to tell me about the death, of SIDS, of a friend's infant daughter.

"What it is, Mom?" Sam said.

What it was, of course, was that our friend had suffered a loss so terrible that I could not even fathom it. Finding my own baby dead in her crib had been—for months and months—my own worst fear. But my babies, all three of them, were thriving. And my Samuel was about to launch himself into a whole new world: The baby fat was gone, but his amazing sweetness wasn't. He looked at me with big eyes. "Are you okay, Mom?" he said. "Do you need a hug?"

My mother and my mother-in-law were right, as usual: in this case, that Sam deserved a mother who paid attention to him now and then. So the next day I got my Mom act together and actually started planning his birthday party. One thing I knew I *didn't* want to do was what we'd done the year before, when I was massively pregnant with the twins and Sam turned four and, just before all Sam's little friends were scheduled to arrive at the house for the first party event—a backyard treasure hunt that didn't work out because the bugs got into the Mars Bars and packages of M & Ms that we'd strategically placed in the backyard under the hot sun—I got a call from a literary agent in New York to whom I had sent some of my short stories, who told me, and I quote, "I'm sorry, Jennifer, but I just don't see that your work really *goes* anywhere," which devastated me so much that when the doorbell started ringing five minutes later, and very small boys bearing brightly wrapped packages began to race through the house, the birthday boy's enormous mother sat on the sofa, having a panic attack.

I also had no intention of paying some service—a restaurant, say, or a caterer—to put on the event. Which left me at square one. Plus I couldn't bake worth a damn.

Then I remembered my mother's ice cream roll. My father's mother, Helene, had given Mom the recipe, and it was, and is, among the most delicious desserts I've ever tasted. Here's what Mom told me when I called her for the recipe:

"Ready? The ingredients are 5 eggs, separated; ½ cup powdered sugar; and 2 tablespoons cocoa. That's it. Easy. Now what you do is beat the egg yolks and sugar together for at least five minutes. Add the cocoa and the stiffly beaten egg whites—yes, you have to beat the egg whites *before* you add them in. Spread the whole *megillah* into a shallow, ten-by-fifteen-inch pan (the pan should be well buttered and sprinkled with flour). Bake it for about five minutes in a hot oven—I'd say about 400 degrees? Remove it from the oven, and turn it out on a piece of waxed paper sprinkled with sugar. Now this is the tricky part—not really tricky, but listen closely, okay? While the cake mixture is still hot, you need to roll it up, along with the waxed paper, and *then* cover it with a damp washcloth. This cools it down. *Then* you unroll it. *Then* you cover it with ice cream. Smooth the ice cream out. Then roll the whole thing back up again, and stick it in the freezer."

She continued: "Don't forget Grandma Helene's hot fudge sauce. Of course, Grandma herself never made any of this. Do you remember Jesse? That wonderful old black man? He really did all the cooking. I don't know where Grandma got all her recipes. After all, she didn't do the cooking. I think when she was younger, she was depressed, only of course in those days no one went into therapy. It just wasn't *done.* I think that's why your father is so quiet. Don't tell her I said so."

"Is this something I can make?"

"Would I give you a recipe that wasn't easy?" she said. "You'll need 1½ cups of confectionery sugar; 2 ounces of bitter chocolate; ½ cup milk, give or take a splash; 2 tablespoons of butter; 1 teaspoon vanilla. You melt the chocolate and butter on low so you don't burn them, then add the milk slowly, because you don't want a watery consistency or a gloppy one; then add the vanilla. Cook until it's smooth and thick but not *too* thick because then it won't spread properly. And is it true what your sister told me that she used to sneak out of the house in the middle of the night to go *horseback* riding with those horrible hippie friends of hers?"

Well, yes, it was, but I didn't want to go into it. It was my sister's secret. It was just kind of hard to believe that she'd grown up to be a partner at her fancy-shmancy Wall Street law firm specializing in mergers and acquisitions. Because, after all, she'd done way worse things. We'd *all* done way worse things, like the time that me and my two best friends, Karin and Nina, smoked grass in the parking lot of Langley High School during a school dance, and then went and cut down the American flag . . . or the time I hitchhiked in Georgetown with this cool-looking half-Indian, half-black guy who insisted on buying me a book about Far Eastern meditation techniques and then drove me to his place—only now that I'm thinking about it, I realize that my parents still don't know about that one.

And anyway, that was then. This was now. I was blessed with three children, and all of them, thank God, were loud and healthy. And the biggest one wanted a birthday party.

What I finally decided to do was give Sam a haunted house party. It wasn't an original idea. When I was little, Mom used to tell me a bedtime story about a haunted house party *she'd* gone to when she was little. The main thing I remembered about it was that the children, blindfolded, had been led around the house, where they felt various body parts, most of them made from food. So on the day of Sam's birthday party, I dressed in black, put a streak of baby powder in my graying hair, painted my lips and fingernails black, and generally looked about as bad as I do on a typical Friday afternoon. The kids arrived. One by one, we blindfolded them and, one by one, told them the story of the witch who used to live in our house and eat little boys. Then we led them to the kitchen, where, on the table, they touched the dead boys' guts (cold spaghetti), brains (over-ripe skinned pineapple), hair (from the barber shop down the road), and eyeballs (skinned grapes). This, of course, gave us the opportunity to scare the crap out of the ones we didn't like—the little brat, for instance, who, whenever he played at our house, routinely "hid" someplace and wouldn't come out, rendering Sam ballistic with anxiety. We *really* laid it on thick for him. Not really, of course! We are responsible, reasonable people. We merely tied his blindfold a little too tight. And when we were all done with the tour of the body parts, we gave the boys ice cream roll with hot fudge sauce, and Sam opened his presents.

Two weeks later, Rose and Jonathan turned one, and I made another of my mother's really really easy-bake ice cream concoctions. This was one she learned from the woman we all called Nanny, Rose Zacks, who'd been my mother's baby nurse, in the days when people had baby nurses. It was the first fancy dessert my mother ever made, and it is as delicious as the most labor-intensive double-chocolate-parfait-truffle-apricot-cake. Here's the recipe:

Beat three egg whites until stiff. Add a teaspoon of cream of tartar and beat. Gradually add a cup sugar. Smash twelve saltines (with a hammer if necessary). Add the smashed-up saltines and about a half a cup of either almonds or pecans to the stiff egg white mixture. Bake in a greased pie dish in a preheated 350-degree oven for half an hour. Cool. Then spread with ice cream and top with fresh fruit.

My mother didn't make it to the twins' first birthday party. She was in the hospital, my father and my brother by her side. My father didn't make it either. He was too busy pacing the halls. But my mother-in-law came. I told her that a part of me still didn't believe that Mom was sick. She said she understood. She said that a part of her still didn't believe that her husband, Stanley, was dead. "For months after his death, I prayed that I'd dream of him," she told me, "and I never did. I never saw him in my dreams. But now, every now and then, I know he's watching over me—that he's watching over all of us. He knows about the children—his grandchildren—and he's glad that you're their mother."

"I don't know—," I said.

"I know," Grandma Lola assured me. "Just look at them! They're the cream in my iced tea!" And I looked over and saw the twins chasing each other around the kitchen table, and Sam, lying on the floor, letting them crawl over him. All three were covered with ice cream and surrounded by presents— books and tapes from Grandma Lola, clothes from my mother, funny hats and wooden blocks and a hand-made wall hanging.

"Do I have something to *kvell* about or do I have something to *kvell* about?" Grandma Lola said. "Just tell me one thing, Jennifer. What are they going to want for Hanukkah?"

NINE

My Husband, the Gourmet

SHORTLY AFTER I'D FINISHED sandblasting the last of Grandma's long-congealed hot fudge sauce from the kitchen floor—which is to say some weeks after the last of the birthday wrapping paper had been shredded up into zillions of little scraps that had managed to float into every corner of the house—I discovered my husband sitting at the kitchen table surrounded by cookbooks, muttering something that sounded like, "What the hell is kiwi balsamic vinegar?"

"We don't have it," I said.

"What about white miso?"

"Ditto."

"Dried porcini mushrooms?"

"Sorry."

"How the hell am I supposed to make dinner when we don't have any of the ingredients?"

My husband, to give credit where credit is due, is a truly terrible cook—but at least he's *interested*. The reason he's such a truly terrible cook is that he almost never cooks—and when he does, he tends to choose complicated recipes with lots of separate steps, each of which requires a different kind of saucepan, like the one he tackled that night. It was an eggplant, kasha, and ground meat recipe, and by the time he'd finished making it, the top of the stove and inside of the oven were coated with grease, eeny-weeny bits of half-cooked foods were embedded in the grain of the cabinets, dirty dishes were overflowing the sink, and everything that had once been inside the refrigerator was outside the refrigerator, melting. Not that I minded spending the better part of the following day on my hands and knees, scraping up burned garlic cloves.

In addition to not having had enough practice, my husband is handicapped, culinarily, by his dependence on cookbooks. He is, in fact, incapable of functioning without following each and every step, ingredient by ingredient. When he makes Kraft macaroni and cheese, for example, he carefully measures the milk. ("The directions on the box say *half a cup*. You can't just splash the milk in and hope that you get the right amount!") My own approach, needless to say, is different. In fact, I don't recall EVER using a cookbook. ("Yeah, and you can tell, too.") I cook the way all the women in my family cook—using the everything-but-the-kitchen-sink method, combined with emergency long-distance phone calls.

But it wasn't until after we were married that I caught onto my husband's cookbook dependence. This is because, during our premarital sex stage, we mainly ate out. And I daresay that, had I known of my husband's cookbook dependence earlier, I may have thought twice before I agreed to stand with him under the *chuppah,* while the rabbi droned on and on, reading from a small spiral notebook in which he'd penned his endless, and not very interesting, thoughts about marriage, while all our guests, sitting in pretty white chairs on the lawn, fell asleep. But like many a love-struck newlywed before me, I was blind to my loved one's shortcomings. The proverbial scales didn't fall from my eyes (a really disgusting image that still doesn't make sense to me) until the first season of our marriage, when we were living in Los Angeles, and my husband decided that he, and he alone, was going to make our dinner for Rosh Hashanah (the Jewish New Year).

It was early fall, and we were preparing for Rosh Hashanah by discussing our different views of religious commitment and obligation. If I recollect correctly, that particular conversation went something like this: "Why are you such a jerk?" "Why are you so sensitive?" "Why are you looking at me that way?" "Why can't you be rational?" "Oh yeah, well what's that stuff on your

nose?" and so on, until we resolved our differ-
ences in the manner of most newlyweds, by deciding never to have sex again.

Actually, it wasn't long after we'd moved to Los Angeles for my husband's career (a move that foreshadowed our later move to Washington for my husband's
career, which itself foreshadowed a yet later move, for
my husband's career—but I'm getting ahead of myself), that I started to feel sick, which was the primary
reason that I'd allowed my husband to take over the
preparation of our holiday dinner to begin with. Because even *before* we were married, we'd fallen into this
typical sexist she-does-the-cooking-and-the-cleaning-
and-the-gardening-and-the-accounting-and-the-
garbage-and-the-sewing-and-the-thank-you-note-writing
/he-does-the-*New York Review*-reading division of labor, so I didn't have a lot of confidence that my husband could indeed pull off an edible meal. Fortunately
Binky, who then lived in San Francisco, was coming
for the holiday, and she *is* a good cook. So rather than
struggle to produce a decent dinner in our extremely
ill-equipped kitchen, I was able to sit back, relax, and
bask in my low-level meningitis.

Why, you may ask, was I not feeling well? Was it the
usual combination of hypochondria and self-pity? Or
was it that I had left a rent-stabilized apartment in
Manhattan, all my friends, and my psychoanalyst, in
order to live in a place where all the women were five-
foot ten-inch blonde goddesses, and all the men were

Harvard-educated sit-com writers, just so my husband could start his legal career off right by clerking for a judge who happened to be a dead ringer for Sandra Day O'Connor? Was it, too, that though I had agreed, in principle, to go to Los Angeles, envisioning myself hanging out at beachside cafés with extremely good-looking and well-placed men who wanted to hire me to write movies for a hundred thousand dollars a pop or thereabouts, I in fact didn't know anyone and was so lonely that I'd started hanging out with Shelby, the small, pale, bald man who lived with his collection of nude Barbie dolls with shaved heads in the one-room apartment down the hall?

Indeed, my new husband, whom I'd married for all the right reasons, was never home. He was always "downtown" (a misnomer in Los Angeles), in "chambers," "writing" "briefs" for "the Judge." Which meant that I had to go out and get my own damn job. It was either that or live on a single modest salary and pal around with Shelby and his bald, naked Barbie dolls. Which is how I found myself, one day, chatting with the editor of *Bon Appetit*. I told him that food was my greatest passion in life, followed by Shakespeare, French poetry, and the delta blues. So I lied. I got the job, didn't I?

Even though I kept making a mash of the recipes, it was a great job. Every day at eleven, and then again around three, the food editors would "test" recipes in the magazine's elaborate test kitchens, and the staff would be called in to "taste" the results. My very first day on the job, I was asked to "taste" salmon mousse, roast wild duckling on a bed of herbs, acorn squash and sweet potato soup, and mocha layer cake. I started putting on weight about three seconds later. After about a month, all the chic clothes that I'd brought with me from New York started getting tight, and my husband went around telling people that I was paid to eat.

Despite my hearty appetite, I distinctly didn't feel well, and I had no one, such as my psychoanalyst, to complain to. Meanwhile, the New Year was approaching, and so was my sister. Perhaps because I was coming home every day with tales of triple cheese tarts bathed in a vinaigrette of olive oil, rosemary, basil, and roasted shallots, or perhaps because he wanted to show off, my husband took it into his head that he could make cornish game hens with prune-apricot chutney and Mediterranean-roasted new potatoes. He thought that cornish game hens with prune-apricot chutney and Mediterranean-roasted new potatoes would be more exciting than the standard High Holiday pot roast or roasted chicken. Plus, he said, he was going to make it kosher (in honor of the holiday). He was so sure he could handle this recipe that he didn't ask me to do anything to help him, except buy all the ingredients, and explain to him what exactly a cornish game hen was. ("It's a little chicken," I said. "No, really," he said.)

Fortunately, by the time it was time to start cooking, my sister had arrived. I was lying in bed, wondering whether I had the energy to paint my fingernails, when, from the kitchen, I heard my husband and my sister talking in very loud voices:

"The recipe says to use butter, but butter isn't kosher with meat," my husband said.

"So use margarine or olive oil instead."

"But the recipe specifically calls for *butter*."

"So use butter."

"But then it won't be kosher."

"God will strike you dead."

"And look at this. The recipe calls for stale French bread, cubed. What does 'cubed' mean?"

"What do you think it means?"

"Did Jennifer remember to get the stale French bread?"

"There's some bread here."

"But that's *sour*dough bread. The recipe doesn't say *sour*dough bread. The recipe says stale French bread. Why didn't Jennifer buy stale French bread? I told her specifically to buy stale French bread. This bread isn't even very stale."

"Leave it out on the window sill for ten minutes."

"The recipe says that the bread has to soak for a full two hours."

"Why don't you go soak your head for a full two hours?"

"What is it with all the women in your family?"

Which brings up the subject: What *is* it with all the

women in my family or, at the very least, me? To
this day I don't know why I spent most of my
twenties having a prolonged nervous breakdown.
My mother and father, unlike the mother and father in
Mary Karr's absolutely stunning *The Liars' Club,* didn't
drink and cuss and fight, and leave me in the care of
baby-sitters who forced me to suck their dicks when I
was eight years old and home sick with the flu. (When
I read the reviews of *The Liars' Club,* I immediately fell
into a fit of jealous rage, wishing that it had been I, and
not Mary Karr, who had had the nightmarish childhood, thereby enabling me, and not Mary Karr, to
write a best-selling memoir about it.) But my parents
didn't expose me to danger of any kind, unless you
count the fancy girls' summer camp that they sent me
to summer after summer, the same one where Mom
had triumphed on the athletic fields but where I was
such a miserable failure that the head counselors are
still holding me up as an example of what not to be. I
still remember jumping up and down in my white
Keds under the Team Tree, trying to demonstrate that I
was, after all, a normal girl who only wanted her team
to win, and not a mosquito-bite-scratching Nazi-ob-
sessed weirdo. I hated sports. I didn't have team spirit. I
didn't even have *camp* spirit. I wanted to blow the
whole fucking camp to smithereens, sending little
bloody bits of all those athletic girls with good attitudes
and strong hand-and-eye coordination sky-high, along
with their tennis rackets, white middy blouses, blue

shorts, and "dress whites." All I wanted was to be back where I belonged, at home, wandering with my dog, George, through the woods near our house, evading the storm troopers.

"Nothing's with the women in my family," I heard my sister snort. "What's your problem?"

"Let me remind you that you are in my home."

"Some home."

Our apartment was in fact so seedy that when my mother came out to visit us the following summer, she refused to sleep there, insisting that we get her a hotel room. It was on the top floor of a prewar building that looked designed to collapse at the first earthquake tremors. And though we were in L.A., where it sometimes seemed as if everyone drove a Porsche and had a house or two in Malibu, our fellow tenants were poor. Many were refugees—old ladies with thick Eastern European accents who sat together on the front steps, talking about the grandchildren who never visited, or, sometimes, about the War. All but Hilda. Hilda never hung out on the steps. Hilda had survived Dachau, and although she wore the same gray dress day after day, she was always doing laundry. You have to understand that there was only one washing machine and one dryer for the whole building, so competition for these machines was fierce. God forbid you should arrive in the laundry room a second or two before her. I once made the mistake of removing Hilda's not-quite-dry laundry from the dryer (she had run out of quarters hours earlier). She tracked me to my door, where she cursed me out in Yiddish until I broke down and begged her forgiveness.

The conversation in the kitchen continued:

"Why don't you see if you can do something useful, like run out and buy some stale French bread? There's a bakery a few blocks away."

"I can't believe my sister married you."

But it was really just a dispute over clashing cooking styles. My sister's, like mine, is more free-wheeling, while my husband's, as I've already described, is not. Plus there's the matter of my sister's name. My sister's *real* name is Barbara, but I still can't call her anything but Binky, even though she has promised to cut me and my children out of her will should I ever so much as drop a dumb hint about her childhood nickname to anyone she knows. In a word, it's hard to have a serious conversation about *anything*, including food, with a person called "Binky," even if the Binky in question is my Binky, who is so smart she scares people.

But after a while, the shouting coming from the roach clubhouse—I mean the kitchen—stopped altogether, prompting me to skip my afternoon fingernail-painting plans and go in and investigate. Stuff was everywhere—bread and bread crumbs and olive oil and a bag of prunes and another of apricots and aluminum foil and wine and croutons—and my sister and my husband were standing on either side of the half-counter, talking about the law.

"But when former prosecutors become judges, they tend to rule harshly on matters pertaining to evidentiary rulings, especially the admissibility of certain kinds of evidence, for example, in the recent Sixth Circuit case, presided over, I believe, by a Reagan appointee . . ."

Like nearly everyone else in my family, Binky is a lawyer. Which means that any meal or preparation thereof in my house eventually becomes a discussion of really really really boring legal shit that nobody wants to hear about ever, under any circumstances whatsoever. I didn't even bother reminding Binky and my husband that there was cooking to do. I was just too depressed. I mean, here I was, a million miles away from my old life in New York, so lonely that I'd started making eyes at Shelby, surrounded by old ladies with bad memories, and on top of everything else, I was gaining weight. I could no longer squeeze into my blue jeans, not to mention the bright red miniskirt I'd bought in an East Village boutique a few weeks before I'd so foolishly agreed to go through with the wedding ceremony that my mother had spent the entire previous year obsessing about. How was I going to meet hip people who wore cool-guy sunglasses and hung around with Jack Nicholson if, on top of everything else, I was fat?

"I don't feel well," I said.

"Why don't you go for a run or something?" my husband said.

"I don't need exercise," I said. "I think what I need is a lobotomy."

"Stop moping around, and go out and take a run," he said. "You'll feel better."

"I'll go with you," Binky said.

Though by this time I felt like a swollen tick, I changed into my running shorts, which fortunately had a well-worn elastic band. My husband, meantime, would just have to get on with the meal as best he could. The New Year, after all, was coming. Binky had come all the way from San Francisco to spend the holiday with us. We were *supposed* to be examining our minds and hearts and souls in an effort to make up for our bad deeds of the past year and do better for the coming one. But all I could think was that I'd made a big mistake. I didn't want to be in Los Angeles; I didn't want to be married; I wasn't at all sure that I liked my new husband. If I'd had even an ounce of courage or imagination, I would have stayed in my tenement apartment with its sloping floors and pressed tin ceiling, hung out with artists and musicians, and, for good measure, had a lesbian affair or two. Maybe then I would have had something to write about.

Binky and I trotted out of the sagging old apartment building, past the old women sitting in the cool of the late afternoon, and down the block. We'd gone maybe a quarter mile when I became winded and had to slow down from my usual slow trot to a ridiculously slow trot.

"Come on!" Binky yelled from up ahead. "What's the problem?"

Mind you, my sister has asthma. Most road kill moves faster than she does. But on that day, I could barely keep up.

"I think I have a brain tumor," I said.

"Maybe," she said.

"And I'm getting fat," I said.

"Maybe a little."

"What do you think's wrong with me?"

"The lobotomy will probably take care of it."

Binky slowed down, and by forcing myself to think of the fat cells that I was jiggling off, I managed to complete the entire not-quite-a-mile run. When we got back to the apartment, a miracle had taken place. An aroma not unlike that of roasting chicken filled our two small rooms; something wonderfully wonderful was bubbling in the broiler; and a heap of fresh vegetables glistened in a bowl on the countertop. My husband stood before the stove, humming.

"Good run?" he said.

"So-so. Your wife is getting fat," Binky said.

"It's all those feedings they have at work," my husband said. "Jennifer has the perfect job. She's paid to eat."

In addition to Cornish Game Hens with Prune-Apricot Chutney, my husband made Mediterranean-Roasted New Potatoes and a medley of sautéed vegetables, and though the kitchen was so filthy that I in fact didn't finish cleaning it until many months later, when I experienced a textbook case of nesting instinct that had me down on my hands and knees scrubbing behind the refrigerator, the meal my husband made was delicious.

These are the recipes he used.

My Husband's High Holy Days Cornish Game Hens

2 medium-sized kosher cornish game hens
1 cup pitted prunes, chopped
1 cup dried apricots, chopped
1 loaf stale French bread
½ cup olive oil
2 tablespoons apricot jam
1 tart apple, finely chopped
1 jar store-bought chutney

Wash and pat dry hens. Tear bread into small pieces and soak in olive oil. Combine bread mixture, chopped pitted prunes, chopped dried apricots, and lightly sauté until bread is golden-crisp. Remove from heat. Pack hens with bread mixture. Combine apricot jam, chopped apple, and jar of chutney, and pour over hens. Bake at 350 degrees until done, about ninety minutes.

Mediterranean-Roasted New Potatoes
That Even My Husband Can Make

6 or 7 medium to large new potatoes, peeled and
 chopped into 1-inch cubes
4 or 5 garlic cloves, finely chopped
1 cup olive oil

Preheat oven to broil. Parboil potatoes until slightly
tender, about fifteen minutes. Place in shallow baking
dish and toss with mixture of garlic and olive oil. Broil
on medium, about six inches from heating element,
turning often, until done—about thirty minutes.

For the vegetables, my husband chopped up all the
veggies I'd bought—red and green bell peppers, onions,
pea pods, and carrots—and sautéed them in a mixture
of Oriental sesame oil, vegetable oil, soy sauce, and
fresh chopped ginger. When the vegetables were
cooked through but still crisp, he added a handful of
shelled peanuts.

The three of us took turns in the cruddy, crumbling
bathroom showering, and then we met, in our good
clothes, at the table that had been set with our best
Corning Ware dishes. The food was in fact so good—as
was the bottle of wine that my sister had thrown in as a
little Rosh Hashanah present—that we sort of forgot to
go to synagogue that night.

Two days later, the three of us got up early and
drove to San Pedro, where we took an early-morning

boat to Catalina Island, a beautiful, wild place with almost no cars. I would have enjoyed the crossing more—I'd planned on sitting on the open deck, a book propped open on my lap—had I not been booting the entire time. The return trip was no better. And then I started getting seasick on dry land. I went back to work, and my clothes got tighter and tighter, and even though I continued praying, nearly every day, to the porcelain goddess, I didn't lose weight. By Thanksgiving, I was convinced that there was something *in* there and I didn't have long to live.

Finally I made an appointment to see a gynecologist. The nurse who listened as I described my alarming symptoms told me to make pee-pee in a cup. She took my pee-pee and plopped it in a test tube with some blue stuff. Then she told me that I was pregnant.

Boy, did I feel dumb. Mind you, when I was in high school, my mother was president of the Washington, D.C., branch of Planned Parenthood. She entertained us during dinner with stories about troublesome IUDs and girls who forgot to take their birth control pills. So I should have known better. I should have known, indeed, that owning a misplaced birth control device can and often does lead to morning sickness. A few weeks later, my belly popped out. I was now expecting, and people I'd never before met started doing things like patting me on the belly and asking, "Is it a boy or a girl?"

(The correct answer to this question is: "Yes.")

The old ladies who lived in our building took a new interest in me too. I heard all the stories of all their pregnancies—in Krakow before the war, and in Hamburg, and in Detroit and Buffalo. I heard about the children they'd lost and the children who never visited them. I heard about the children who had died. I heard about the children who'd disappeared. The children who never came back from the camps. The children who never returned from the front. They nagged me to drink enough milk and yelled at me when I carried grocery bags. "You're carrying high, it's a boy," they said. Or: "You're carrying low, it's a girl." I didn't have the heart to tell them that I wasn't at all sure that I wanted a baby. I didn't have the heart to tell them that, more and more often, I dreamed that I was being carted off to jail.

When, in August, we brought Sam home from the hospital, the old ladies were waiting. Marie gave Sam a soft white towel and washcloth; Lillian gave him a basket; Francis gave him a baby bottle; Yetta gave him a rattle; Hilda gave him a five-dollar bill. "How's the baby?" they'd say.

The baby? Some baby. The little monster we'd made was up every night, night after night, shrieking his bald little head off, balling up his fists, and spitting up on me.

"Fine," I'd say.

"Isn't he beautiful?" the old ladies cooed.

Was he? I'd look down into his little face and see sheer, naked panic. The kid *knew* that I was completely and utterly incapable of raising him. I gazed down on him and saw the years and years of future psychotherapy bills we'd be paying. I figured that they'd start when Sam was old enough to talk and end, finally, a few years after I hit menopause.

"Is he sweet, or is he sweet?" the old ladies would say.

They begged me to let them hold him, and they sang songs to him in Russian and Polish and Yiddish, and they clucked and cooed while he fussed and screamed. And God! I loved him so! And the old ladies knew it. They could glance at me and see how swollen, how flushed I was, with this new, precious thing. He was so beautiful, so tiny, so innocent—and he was mine, and I had *made* him! He was perfect and lovely and filled with the pulse of creation itself. And we were going to raise him up right, with love and great gentleness, and he was going to be a musician, or a doctor, or a teacher.

The old ladies checked up on us every day. And then, when Sam was six weeks old, my husband and I packed up our stuff, waved goodbye, and moved to Washington.

Every year while my husband is preparing our Rosh Hashanah dinner, we talk about that first year of our marriage, when I was pregnant with Sam in that seedy apartment in that sagging building filled with Jewish refugees.

"Those old women were so kind to us," my husband says.

And I wonder if any of them would remember us, if we were ever to return.

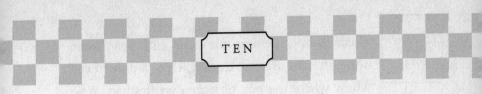

TEN

Spilled Beans

SINCE THAT DAY that we'd brought Sam home from the hospital, our world had changed in a big way. Our crummy apartment had given way to a house with a yard, a tree-lined street, kids on bicycles, and neighbors who drove minivans. Now we had a mortgage of our very own, and a living room decorated in a traditional *enfant* scheme anchored by a collapsing vintage playpen. The biggest change, of course, was that our precious first-born baby boy, the child we called "Samuel" because the name means "God has heard," had long since graduated from mushed-up bananas mixed with Gerbers rice cereal.

In fact, he was onto frozen waffles. He'd discovered

them during the autumn of his fifth year, some time after he started kindergarten. I didn't even know where the box of frozen waffles had come from—God knows that *I* wouldn't buy them—but for weeks on end, there they were, in our freezer, disappearing one by one. Then one day they were gone. The next morning, Sam woke me up at dawn, wailing about how I didn't love him anymore. "What?" I said. "Because if you loved me," he said, "you'd let me have waffles!" And he burst into tears.

My husband pointed out that we were, in fact, out of frozen waffles because Sam had eaten all of them. But Sam only wailed more. "Be quiet or you'll wake up the babies," I said. Sam's wails grew louder. "And that's another thing," he cried. "You love the babies more than you love *me!*"

Well, yes, there was, at that moment, some truth to this. Rose and Jonathan were both asleep. Sam was spewing snot on my face. It wasn't much of a contest. On the other hand, I knew from my years in therapy, during which I retrieved all kinds of odd moments from my own dysfunctional childhood, that, to this day, my father preferred my siblings to me for a variety of reasons or even if he didn't, I thought he did, which amounted at the time to the same thing and—and this is the important part—that's why I ended up crazy to begin with. In other words, as I lay in bed hoping that Sam would get the hint and go away, it occurred to me that one of the ill effects of being in therapy for a long time, and changing therapists every few years as you move from town to town, is not only that you dwell on all your old aches and pains, lugging them around in your own set of ratty luggage like a bag lady on a bad trip and boring all your friends to tears, but also that you tend to think that every little blip that crosses your mind is not only significant, but ought to be shared, even if those blips, taken together, don't cohere. Which is to say that as Sam stood over me, spewing snot and whining about frozen waffles, I worried that his little brains were already so badly scrambled by bad mothering that it was only a matter of minutes before he started taking drugs and wearing torn black jeans while he made plans to contract a sexually transmitted disease.

"At least Grammy loves me," Sam said as he buried his little head in my neck. "She promised she'd buy me waffles as soon as she feels better." Then, as I began to work on a fresh ulcer, he burst into a new round of sobs.

One thing was sure: He was going into a weird food stage. He'd gone through a few already. When he was just beginning to toddle, for example, he ate two or three bananas every day. Sometimes all he would eat, on any given day, were bananas. I figured that at the very least, he got his potassium. But now he refused to eat whole categories of foods, such as: meat, fish, chicken, vegetables, fruit, whole-grain anything, pasta, cheese, eggs, milk, or yogurt, including the kind that has so much sugar in it that it tastes like custard.

Meanwhile, I knew that it was a good idea to avoid food struggles with him. Just about every parenting book will tell you not to force your children to eat everything on their plate—they'll only end up spitting their half-chewed chicken and peas into their napkins, as I myself did—but I found it almost impossible to restrain myself.

So the next time I was at the pediatrician's office for our biweekly visit, I flipped through the waiting room's collection of dog-eared parenting magazines, in search of some answers. But this was a nonstarter. Though there was lots of advice on the subject, I just couldn't take the photographs of all those clean children eating, for instance, grilled shrimp on a bed of lightly sautéed vegetables. This kind of dining experience was simply beyond my comprehension, and I knew from experience that Sam could not tolerate a meal in which the separate food categories touched each other.

In desperation, I turned to my friends and neighbors to see if any of them had come up with creative ways to shovel a little nutritious food into their children. At first everyone told me the same thing: peanut butter and jelly. But little by little they shared their trade secrets.

Here are their recipes:

Pizza (Courtesy of Elizabeth Patton)

Ingredients: small-sized Boboli pizza shells, shredded cheese, chopped tomatoes, chopped black olives, ground beef.

On a beautiful, warm, fragrant fall day—the kind of day that had you had eight hours of sleep last night instead of barely six, would make you think that you were living inside a ViewMaster—preheat oven to 350 degrees. While Sam is outside in the middle of the street having a giant screaming match with the neighbors' kids, throw some chopped ground beef in a heavy skillet and fry, on medium, until done, shaking often to ensure that meat is cooked in little kid-sized grayish-pinkish clumps. When cooked through, arrange meat in a bowl, and set on the countertop. Arrange other ingredients in additional bowls.

Savor this one, fleeting moment of peace: You are alone in your kitchen, just you and Nina Totenberg, who obviously doesn't have kids, because if she did, she wouldn't be out there, having this absolutely fabulously glamorous and successful career, and what's so great about her, anyway? Can't she just shut up already? Wonder when you'll find the time to go see Mom in the hospital. Strike that. The truth is, you don't want to go to the hospital anymore. You're tired of going to the hospital, tired of sitting by the bed, tired of holding her hand. You don't *like* to hold her hand. You can't stand to hear the retching noises she makes, or to see how scrawny she's gotten under her nightgowns. You're not a nurse, you're not a doctor: You're her daughter, and you don't want to see it anymore. The EKG machine; the IVs. How does your brother take it? He spends much more time with her than you do. What kind of infection does she have this week, anyway? Every other week, it's something new and different—lining of the heart, the liver, the lungs, what next?—that lands her hooked up to intravenous antibiotics. Frankly, you're tired of pretending that all you feel for her is worry, when in fact sometimes you just wish your stupid husband would just go ahead and get a teaching job *anywhere*—in West Butt Freeze, Alaska, or Nowheresville, Louisiana—so you could move away and put this whole tedious family drama behind you. All that talk about "making it" and "fighting" when the truth is—and everyone but Dad knows it—that Dad'll be remarried before you can say "young second wife and she's not even Jewish."

Why are you such a bitch? Dad's suffering, too— any half-wit can see it: the hooded eyes, the deepening lines, the way he paces back and forth like a soldier in a nursery rhyme. Go to front door. Yell: *Suppertime!* When this summons elicits no response, yell: *Right now young man!* When Sam at last drags himself away from the other kids, notice that he's covered in: What *is* that, anyway? How can any one person be so filthy? Do you have to touch him? And what do you do if, God forbid, he tries to sit on any of your furniture?

Insist that he change his clothes and wash his
hands. Don't look too closely. When his hands
are "washed," let him fix his own mini-pizza.
Place in oven. Explain to him that it will be another
ten minutes until his pizza is cooked, and that *no,* he
may not watch TV while he's waiting for dinner. No,
you *really* mean it this time. Did I say "yes" or did I say
"no"? What does "no" mean, anyway? I don't *care* if all
the other kids watch Fox. I don't care if Grammy lets
you watch television at her house this is my house do
you understand young man? Grab Budweiser from
back of refrigerator. Open and drink. While Sam
watches TV upstairs, wonder if you're developing a
drinking problem. Serve pizzas warm, with chocolate
milk.

Noodles au Gratin (Courtesy of Nicholas Greenfield)

Ingredients: 1 large-sized box Kraft Macaroni and
Cheese, milk, butter, one box spinach fettucine, freshly
grated parmesan cheese, fresh basil.

Cook macaroni and cheese according to directions
on box. Notice that Jonathan is now tall enough to get
into cutlery drawers. Carefully extract steak knife from
his hand; calmly explain to him that steak knives are
dangerous. Tell him that biting is not allowed. Tell him
that biting *hurts.* Tell him that supper is *coming*—you
only have two hands. Tell him that biting *hurts.* Open

refrigerator door, bashing it into Rose's face. Scoop her up. Tell Jonathan that biting really *hurts,* you mean it, and furthermore, isn't it time he learned to say something other than "ugh" and "erg"? At what point do signs of autism appear? When mac 'n' cheese is ready, call Sam and his best friend Nicholas in for lunch. Lurch for ringing phone. Maybe it's an editor at the *New Yorker* telling you that they loved that story you sent them eight months ago that still hasn't been returned. But no. It's AT&T calling. Tell the AT&T lady that it's lunchtime, but you'd be happy to call her back at her home while she's serving her family dinner. Slam down phone. At least Mom is back home again, her infection, whatever it was this time, under control. Place twins in high chairs; put bowls of macaroni and cheese before them, carefully avoiding watching them while they eat. Ask big boys to sit at table. Place bowls of macaroni and cheese before them. Listen while your son's best friend Nicholas explains, in highly rational terms, why he simply can't eat mac 'n' cheese: At his house, he has homemade pasta with freshly grated parmesan cheese and basil. Listen as Sam joins in. *Neither* of them can eat this baby junk. Only *babies* eat mac 'n' cheese. Mac 'n' cheese is for *morons.* Return mac 'n' cheese to saucepan. In large, heavy pot boil water; dump fettucine in; when fettucine is cooked, drain and rinse. Serve warm, with freshly grated parmesan cheese, fresh basil, and chocolate milk on the side.

Thrice-Stuffed Baked Potatoes with Vegetarian Baked Beans (My Own Recipe)

Ingredients: large baking potatoes, cream cheese, vegetarian baked beans.

Explain to Sam that Nicholas can't come over today, but that his mother has invented a new recipe specially for Nicholas called thrice-stuffed baked potatoes. Tell him that Nicholas eats thrice-stuffed baked potatoes every single night. Tell him that even though Nicholas eats ham, you don't. Tell him that he cannot have pepperoni pizza for dinner tonight or any night. Tell him that different people have different house rules. Tell him that when he's a grownup, he can decide for himself whether to eat pepperoni pizza for dinner instead of thrice-stuffed baked potatoes. Tell him that it's not polite to go around telling people that Jesus was a man, not God. Tell him that different people have different beliefs, and that the important thing is that we respect one another. Tell him that he cannot, under any circumstances, sleep in his dirty clothes. Tell him that he cannot stay home from school tomorrow. Tell him that he can have a cookie *after* he's eaten his healthy food, not before. Tell him that you don't have any frozen blueberry waffles. Tell him that you do *so* love him, you merely forgot to buy frozen blueberry waffles. Tell him that he cannot, under any circumstances, watch TV while he's waiting for dinner. Tell him that you don't care what his friend Jeffrey has at his house; at *your* house you don't drink Coke with dinner. Tell him that he cannot, under any circumstances, watch TV while he's waiting for dinner. Tell him to stop kicking the table leg. Tell him that Daddy is in Chicago. Tell him that Daddy is trying to get a teaching job. Tell him that you're not angry at Daddy. Tell him that if you move to another city, his collection of dead insects can come too. Tell him you're just tired. Tell him that you don't have PMS. Tell him that Grammy is still sick, but hopefully she'll feel better in a few months. Tell him that her hair will grow back. Tell him to stop fiddling with the can of opened baked beans. Tell him that he'll spill them by mistake. When can lands on floor, spilling contents, say: Now look what you've done. Go to your room and simmer down. Say: No, you can't watch TV.

While Sam is upstairs watching TV, put twins in high chairs, and place an array of food in front of them: sliced bananas, vegetarian baked beans, Cheerios, string cheese. Lurch for phone. Pick it up on the third ring. When Dad tells you that Mom is about to go back into the hospital for another round of chemo, tell him that you're not sure you'll be able to visit. Say: Because my husband is in Chicago at a convention of law school professors, trying to get a teaching job, and I have three kids. Tell Dad that your husband doesn't really want to be a lawyer anymore. Tell him that he won't be home until Monday, and you're losing your mind. Tell him that you'll try to get a baby-sitter. Tell him that you'll do your best. Tell him that you know she wants to see you. Promise Dad that you'll visit Mom in the hospital soon.

Skin potatoes and cook in microwave, about three minutes a side. When potatoes are cooked through, scoop out contents, mix with cream cheese and baked beans, and stuff the mush back inside the potato skins. Zap for an additional minute or so. Serve warm, with chocolate milk.

Messy Mexican Stuff (Courtesy of Janyne Oberdorfer)

Ingredients: ready-to-use flour tortillas, refried beans, black beans, green salsa, shredded cheeses, sour cream.

While singing "the Frito Bandito," invite children into kitchen and announce that you are having a Mexican fiesta! Dance around kitchen, snapping fingers and praying that there is no mini-spy camera hidden in your kitchen cupboards. *I'm the Frito bandito, and I'm here to say* . . . Isn't it amazing how cluttered your mind is with snatches of advertising jingles? Just how many hours of TV did you watch during your own endless suburban childhood? The station wagon. The Monkees. Frye boots. And those horrible long-haired *boys* you had crushes on. And now this: all grown-up, in a kitchen of your own . . . with your very own *microwave!* Breathe deeply as sudden depression descends on you, as if from outer space. Put ingredients in separate bowls. Help various children goop various ingredients atop open tortillas. Zap "finished" tortillas in microwave until ingredients explode, coating inside of microwave with little frazzled bits of refried beans. Start over.

When Dad calls, tell him it's not a good time. When he tells you that Mom's got a new tumor, marvel at how calm he sounds. Calm, certain, level—no wonder he's such a great lawyer, such a forceful advocate. When he tells you that she will never be cured, that all those months of chemotherapy, quite simply, didn't work, notice that you are oddly disengaged. Now, of course, you'll have to rearrange your schedule again, an especially difficult trick to pull off while your husband is out of town. What's wrong with you? Dad sounds awful—like he's half-dead himself. And as for Mom . . . only there's practically no Mom left. Before you hang up, promise Dad that you'll visit as soon as possible.

Call every baby-sitter in town, until you find one who can watch your kids for a few hours so you can go see your mother.

While waiting for baby-sitter to show up, serve tortillas warm, with sour cream, Kleenex, and chocolate milk on side.

Hamburgers with Mashed Potatoes and Peas (Courtesy of Mom)

Ingredients: hamburger meat, baking potatoes, milk, butter, frozen peas, ketchup.

Peel taters and boil them until they're mushy. Drain. Add whole milk, butter, salt and pepper, and mash and mash and mash until there isn't even one single teeny-tiny lump left. Don't forget to make the burgers and the peas.

Arrange hamburger, mashed potatoes, and peas on plate, with enough ketchup to sink a ship. Serve with chocolate milk.

When Sam is seated more or less in his place, half on and half off the chair, explain to him that you've got that mean expression on your face because you're a little worried about Grammy. Explain to him that she's not feeling well. Explain to him that he can have dessert only *after* he's eaten his dinner. Tell him to stop kicking table leg. Tell him to sit on his tuchis. Tell him to use his napkin, not his shirt. Tell him to use his fork, not his fingers. Tell him to stop torturing his brother and sister. Tell him that the dinner is not gross. Tell him that he has to eat most of it. Tell him that dinner is dinner. Tell him that this used to be his very favorite dinner. Tell him not to hide his peas in his napkin. Tell him that he has to at least *try* the burger. Tell him that if he doesn't eat, he can go straight to his room for the rest of the week. On second thought, the rest of the month.

Tell him that there are *no* lumps in the mashed potatoes. Tell him that he's imagining things. Ask him where he came from? Mars? When he bursts into tears, begin to cry. Take him onto your lap. Cry onto his head.

Locate chocolate milk. Pour generously. Locate vodka. Pour generously. Locate Rose and Jonathan. Locate favorite Monkees tape, and play on high volume. When "Mary, Mary," comes on, dance around kitchen wildly, feeling oddly like your fourteen-year-old former self.

Banana Bombs (Courtesy of Nicholas Greenfield)

Ingredients: bananas, peanut butter, raisins

When husband at last gets home from the Chicago job fair, patiently listen to him while he tells you about some bozo professor from some state school you've never heard of. Pretend to be interested while he says: It may not be Harvard, but at least it's a real law school. When he asks you whether you'd be willing to move to the Deep South, say: Are you nuts? Flop on the sofa. You have a stomachache.

When husband asks why you look so awful, start crying for the fortieth time today, and say: It's Mom. Describe how, when you arrived at her house, you found her sitting on a lawn chair in the back yard, gazing out at the trees, with Dad across from her, the two of them in complete silence. Say: Is this really my mother? She looks like she's a hundred years old. She can't hold a pen; can't write a thank-you note; can't talk. Say: She burst into tears the moment I touched her hand. She said she didn't want to suffer any more. She made me promise to help her kill herself at the end.

Say: I promised.

Five minutes later, go into home "office." Call siblings—first Binky, then David, then Amalie.

Say: Mom's had bad news . . .

Say: I know, I know . . .

Afterward, look around at all the ordinary things. The bookshelves. The windows. Your brother, your sisters, they understand. For you are all your mother's children, all blessed and burdened, all filled with sorrow that will not lift.

Let the minutes tick by.

Allow Sam to drag you into kitchen. Tell him that you know he's hungry. Slice open banana, banana-split style. Coat with peanut butter and top with raisins. Say: Roger, over and out, GI Joe to the rescue, fire one, fire two, fire three! Here comes the banana bomb!

Kiss children and serve banana bombs cold, with chocolate milk on side.

ELEVEN

Making Gravy

 I DON'T REALLY KNOW how my mother absorbed the news that she was now, in the cold, clinical language of her doctors, "terminal." All I know is that somehow she did. Her treatments, mercifully, were over. Her doctors had assured her that as time passed and the effects of the chemotherapy lessened, she'd begin to feel better again. They spoke to her of "quality of life" and of probabilities, of hormone inhibitors and mood enhancers. They told her that the torture she'd endured, though it hadn't cured her, had gone a long way toward ridding her body of malignancy, and that she could look forward to a period of relative good health. They said that she should eat and drink anything she liked; that she should enjoy her

friends and her family; that, in short, she should seize the day. But she thought differently. "I don't think I'll be here a year from now," she told each of us in turn.

So when Thanksgiving rolled around, we did what we always did, and flocked out to our parents' house, where my mother, medicated and thinking about dying, sat at her end of the table, in a dream world. She thought that it would be her last Thanksgiving.

So I don't really want to write about Thanksgiving at my parents' house, because even though Mom's hair was beginning to grow in again, in a chicken-feather kind of way, already I'm getting teary and I can't see the computer screen very well. Instead, I want to talk about the time, when Sam was two and the twins were wishes, that my husband and I decided not to go either to my mother's or to Grandma Lola's, but to have Thanksgiving at our house.

Needless to say, this was years before my mother had so much as *heard* of Taxol, let alone cisplatin, carbo-platin, or Cytoxan. At the time, she and Grandma Lola were both fairly new grandmothers; moreover, my husband and I had not yet come to understand that as far as our kid was concerned, we were mere providers of goods and services—food, baths, clean dideys—whereas the grandparents were bearers of treats, angels of delight sent by a kind and just God. So we had Thanksgiving at our house in part because we were then trying to give each of our mothers the same amount of access to their grandson, and we thought that if we had both sides of the family over to our house, both mothers would be happy, thus guaranteeing that they'd both continue to take us out to fabulous dinners at fancy restaurants even if it wasn't our birthdays. Plus, we wanted to circumvent the whole long, tedious, predictable pre-Thanksgiving dialectic, which typically started up around May Day. You know the one: "What do you mean you're going to their house for Thanksgiving? Didn't you go last year? Well, fine, if you feel that way. No, don't worry. Well, I'm certainly not going to make Thanksgiving dinner for just me. No, I *don't* mind skipping Thanksgiving altogether. Now that I'm alone in the world, I've learned how to take care of myself. I'll go to the movies or something." (Sighs loudly.) Followed by: "But all your brothers and sisters will be here. Yes, she's coming in from California. Why? Because she wants to see you, of course! And she wants to see Daddy, too. You mean I didn't tell you? It's nothing, dear, don't worry, only your father's going in for a little exploratory surgery the Monday right after Thanksgiving. Calm down. At his age, you know, things happen. But we're fairly sure that it's nothing. Unless of course it's his prostate or his bowel." (Sobs into the phone.)

This is who we had to our Thanksgiving dinner: my mother and father; my then eighty-eight-year-old grandmother, Helene; my brother, his wife and daughter; my brother's obnoxious friend, a lawyer whom we

invited in the hopes that he and my husband's
sister, who was then single, might like each other,
fall in love, and produce many many many little
children to whom Grandma Lola could give a lot of expensive gifts; my husband's sister; and Grandma Lola.

Like many other first-time Thanksgiving dinner
givers, I was extremely nervous about the prospect of
screwing up. But I discovered that Thanksgiving dinner is easy to prepare. After all, the Pilgrims did it. And
did they have microwave ovens?

The first thing you need is a turkey bag. Let me just
say this: My mother never used turkey bags. And as
I've told my husband countless times, a girl usually
cooks the way her mother cooked, *not* the way her
mother-in-law cooked. So when the various Jewish
holidays come, and my husband expects me to make
homemade gefilte fish and latkes and slippery little delicious meat-filled dumplings, I say (borrowing from
the former mayor of Washington, D.C.): Get over it,
honky. Because my mother didn't cook that way. She's
of *German* Jewish descent, meaning that if it weren't
for the fact of her somewhat prominent nose, she'd actually be Episcopalian. Nor did she use turkey bags.
Grandma Lola, however, uses turkey bags, and much,
much more. Grandma Lola (again unlike my mother)
is a big believer in shortcuts. So when I was preparing
to make this, my first Thanksgiving turkey, Grandma
Lola said: "What's wrong with you, Jennifer? Why
don't you get a turkey bag?" I told her that my mother

didn't use turkey bags, and her turkeys came out just fine. Grandma Lola, who was staying at our house for the holiday, frowned. Then she went upstairs and thumped around for a while. When she returned to the kitchen, she was carrying a Reynolds turkey bag. "I just happened to have one in my cosmetics case," she said.

"Huh?" I said.

"Use it," she ordered.

I'd never seen a turkey bag before. And what it is is: a big plastic bag that you can cook a turkey in, and—and this is the good part—it won't explode in your oven.

Before I even had a chance to read the directions, Grandma Lola had already coated the inside of the bag with flour, melted some margarine in the microwave, shaken a little salt, pepper, and oregano on the bird, coated it with the melted margarine, and stuffed the whole shebang into the bag, and from there, into the oven. "There," she said. Then she taught me how to make gravy. And what she did was: She removed the neck and giblets from the bird, then cooked them in water in a covered saucepan. Then she added chopped-up celery. Then she added some of the drippings from the turkey bag. Finally she added more water, and flour, and chicken broth, and salt and pepper. Then she threw out the neck.

Finally, smiling at Sam, she said: "Guess what? Grandma Lola has a surprise for you!" And she went into her cosmetics bag and pulled out a new four-wheel-drive 4 × 4 vehicle.

A word here, while I'm on the subject, on turkeys. (The kind with feathers, versus the kind you dated before you knew any better.) In my all-four-wheel-drive-vehicle-where-did-you-go-to-law-school-I-went-to-Harvard neighborhood, people would go all gaga over turkey. Specifically what they'd do is order fresh, free-range turkeys for $43.29 a pound at the kind of upscale gourmet stores where the cashiers all look like Italian movie stars.

No, when it comes to turkey, I want something as dead as possible. I mean: these free-range things. Ugh. You can still see the little pockmarks where the feathers have been pulled out. I prefer the kind of turkey that you can buy in your grocer's frozen food case. The kind with its own pop-out thermometer that lets you know when the thing is fully roasted. This is a turkey that you *know* is dead, and, what's more, has been dead, and frozen solid, for a long, long time. The only problem with going this route is that, unless you're my brother's wife and happen to be ridiculously well organized, you will—and this is a promise—become entangled in the pre-Thanksgiving supermarket rush-hour traffic jam. We're talking lots and lots of little old ladies jamming their carts into yours while muttering curses under their breath. We're talking crying kids, and spilled containers of melting ice cream, and deli counter attendants who say: "I've only got two hands, for Christ's sake, don't you people have eyes in your heads?" We're talking about women having breakdowns in front of the yam bins, when they discover that the store is down to its last three yams, and of those, two of them resemble Richard Nixon.

Despite the horrors of grocery shopping, I managed to plan a traditional meal. The turkey; the stuffing; the gravy; the sweet potatoes; mashed potatoes; and creamed spinach. Also salad and apple pie.

I'm not going to give the recipes for the potatoes, because any basic cookbook will include them. But here is my mother's recipe for creamed spinach.

2 tablespoons butter
2 cups whole milk, more or less
Some flour
2 packages frozen spinach, thawed
Nutmeg
Salt and pepper

Melt the butter on low heat. Slowly add a splash of milk, then a tad of flour, then another splash of milk, then another tad of flour, stirring all the while, until you've made a cream sauce. Season with nutmeg, salt, and pepper, testing with finger to make sure that the cream sauce is good. Add the spinach, and stir.

The one really inspired thing I did that particular Thanksgiving, apart from noticing that my brother's obnoxious friend wasn't so much as making eye contact

with my husband's sister, which led me to conclude that it was *not* yet time to start planning the
wedding, was this: I asked one sister-in-law to
provide the dessert, and the other sister-in-law to provide the salad. A potluck Thanksgiving? Why not? I was
still going to be stuck doing the dirty dishes.

"Ta-da!" I said, bringing the bird out. "Happy
Thanksgiving, everyone!" I smiled. I kissed my husband. My father made a blessing. Then we all got down
to business. Well, the bird was marvelous, moist and
juicy, just as Grandma Lola had promised—*and* there
was no unsightly turkey-pan-and-oven mess to clean
up the next day. And a half-hour later, our plates empty
and our bellies full, we sat—my family along with my
husband's—around my dining room table, in utter,
stony silence. It wasn't that no one attempted to make
conversation. Every now and then, someone—usually
my eighty-eight-year-old grandmother, Helene—
would say: "My, isn't this delicious?" Or: "Getting cold
out." Or: "How about those Redskins, huh?" And then
someone would belch. Finally, in desperation, I turned
to my father, and asked him a political question.

"Dad," I said, "what do you think of the president's
domestic policies?"

And off he went! My father is in fact a very smart,
very shrewd man, and like most other Washington an-
imals, he's extremely opinionated and always right. It
would take pages and pages to record all he said about
the president's domestic policies. So for the purposes
of brevity I'll paraphrase:

"Gobble," he said. "Gobble gobble gobble gobble."

This gave the women an opportunity to clear the dishes. Which in turn gave Grandma Lola an opportunity to turn to me and say: "That was really nice. But don't you think it's time to have more children?"

"Beg pardon?" I said.

"Jennifer," she said. "You've got to make gravy while the sun shines."

"What?"

"You've got to turn your oven on."

"Excuse me?"

"Just some fuel for thought."

I returned to the dining room. The men were *still* talking. All of them saying: "Gobble gobble *gobble* gobble gobble."

My mother peered around the corner. "Why don't you two take a walk?" she said. "I'll clean up."

A moment later, Grandma Lola took me aside. "You two go on outside, take a walk," she said. "I don't mind cleaning up."

I remember the long walk my husband and I took around the neighborhood as if it were yesterday. We strolled hand in hand through the cold, crisp November afternoon, gazing now at each other, now at the stark black trees, now at the sky, glowing pink in the west. Really, everything had been okay. The food had been pretty good—completely up to snuff, and I'd even learned a thing or two about turkey bags. And our relatives weren't so bad after all. At least our two mothers

had smiled at each other. At least they *cared*.
Even now, they were side by side in the kitchen,
doing dishes. My grandmother was a living miracle—so old and physically worn down that it was as if
she were wrapped in cotton wool, and yet she was just
as acute as ever, never uttering a word that wasn't posi-
tive. True, my father was odd—but he was lovable in
his own hard-ass way. Okay, so maybe they were all a
little goofy, but I knew, as I'd always known, that if I
were ever in trouble, I could call on any one of them,
and they'd be by my side. Most of all, I'd somehow
married a man whose company I cherished, and together we'd made gravy.

When we got home, the house was still a mess, the
men were still pontificating on the subject of presiden-
tial policies, my brother's obnoxious friend was pound-
ing the table with his fist, and my grandmother, both
my sisters-in-law, and my niece were sitting in silence
in the living room, looking at their feet. But from upstairs! Lo! The sounds of laughter! Our Sam, our pride
and joy, was whooping it up!

I went upstairs. Sam was in his room, sitting in a
pile of brand-new stuff—a couple dozen children's
CDs, his first "My Little Sony" Walkman, a tub of
Play-Doh, a box of sidewalk chalk, a three-foot-long
realistic-looking boa constrictor made of slimy green
rubber, a Barney bedspread, a bright yellow plastic
dump truck, a pair of light-up sneakers, a knight-in-
shining-armor outfit, and a wristwatch in the shape of

a dinosaur—playing with the little white Styro-
foam do-hickeys that fragile objects come packed
in. He was throwing them up in the air and
laughing as they came back down on his head.

"Look Mommy," he said. "Snow."

"Where are Grandma Lola and Grammy?" I said.

He pointed out the door. And then I saw them. My
mother was passed out on the sofa in our little den. My
mother-in-law was snoozing on our bed. They looked
so peaceful, like innocent, slumbering children. I
couldn't imagine my life without them.

TWELVE

Preparation Anxiety

As WINTER MOVED IN, I thanked God that both grandmothers were still with us, even if one of them was not exactly in the best of health. We'd fallen into our cold weather rhythm of school, work, and endless loads of laundry. And then, voilà, things changed. In January, my husband came home from the office and said: "I think I may actually get a job teaching law. How would you feel about moving to Baton Rouge?"

"Where's Baton Rouge?" I said.

"In Louisiana," he said. "It's the state capital."

"Are you shitting me?" I said.

Two weeks later, I found myself sitting under an enormous live oak tree on the campus of Louisiana

State University, praying that my husband would blow the job talk he was in the midst of giving, so that he and I could remain in Washington— where you could, at the very least, get a decent bagel— and my husband could continue spending most of his waking hours strapped to his word processor at the office, writing legal documents, and wondering what had happened to his youthful idealism. It would be bad enough, I thought, to pull up stakes and start all over again in a place where no one understood the meaning of the word *shlepp,* let alone *plotz, meshuggeneh,* and *shtump,* but to have to do it now, when my mother was still so sick, was simply impossible.

The next day, we returned to Washington, where our kids jumped up and down in excitement, threw their little arms around us, and said, "Where are our presents?" And for the next several weeks, my husband and I talked about one thing, and one thing only: other people's sex lives. Just kidding. What we really talked about was whether he'd get the job in Baton Rouge and, if so, whether we'd actually do this ludicrous thing and move to the far ends of the earth where, as everyone knows, everyone is a fascist racist anti-Semite who drives a pickup truck, listens to country western, votes for David Duke, and hunts baby deer.

Then one night while I was trying to extract bubble gum from Sam's hair, my husband put an end to the suspense. He called me from his office and said, "Pack your bags."

"Fuck," I said.

"That's my girl," he said.

"What does *fuck* mean?" Sam said.

Indeed, my husband had been offered a faculty appointment at the LSU law school, in Baton Rouge, Louisiana, which is about as far away as you can get from Washington, D.C., and still be, at least technically, in the continental United States. We'd been told that, in addition to a law school, Louisiana has very large insects, lovely generous people who talk funny and occasionally try to convert the Jews for our own good, humidity so thick it makes you feel that you've been wrapped in hot seaweed, the best jazz and blues in the world, political corruption so smarmy that it has been elevated to an art form, and lots of good eating.

For two or three weeks after the phone call, I alternated between free-floating euphoria and debilitating stomach cramps. Yes, my feelings were mixed. On the one hand, Louisiana would mean having a husband who would actually get to know his children, summers off, and no snow. On the other hand, it meant leaving my friends and neighbors, my house, all my ex-therapists, my extended family, and my mother, who kept cracking jokes about my father's second wife—and it would mean dwelling among southerners, who, as a rule, all looked to me like George Wallace on a bad day. But the handwriting was on the wall. I mean that literally. In his excitement over the prospect of getting a bigger room, Sam had drawn a map of Louisiana in the dining room with the new "erasable" felt-tip pens he'd gotten from Grandma Lola for Hanukkah.

There were layers of memory for me in Washington, layers and layers—after all, I'd grown up there—and it wasn't easy for me to say goodbye to it. I loved our street; I loved our house; I loved the way the light slanted through the trees in the alley behind our windows. I was getting all goopy and sentimental about it, so much so that I was beginning to think that I enjoyed listening to people talk endlessly about the case they'd just finished litigating, the one involving cellular telephone distribution rights in the greater Trenton area. So it didn't help much when, one early evening in spring, Sam packed up his Power Rangers backpack with his blanket, a washcloth, a cloth napkin, his Power Rangers cassette and cassette player, a couple of sticks, and his rubber boa constrictor, and ran away. It was getting dark, and away he went, sauntering off into the great unknown, in a rage over the injustice of my not agreeing to let him have something or another he wanted. A cookie? A swimming pool? A second set of twins? I can't remember. But I admired his spirit, the determination with which he had carried out his threat. By the time I found him (he had run away to his friend Sam Cohen's house, a block away, and was watching TV), half my neighbors were out looking for him. One of them stopped by on her way back to her house to make sure I'd located Sam, and after I explained to her that he was upstairs, chained to his bed until he was old enough to vote, we had the following chat:

Neighbor: How do you feel about moving to Baton Rouge?

Me: Mixed.

Neighbor: Why exactly are you going?

Me: [Long-winded explanation.]

Neighbor: I know your *husband* will be happy, Jen. It's *you* that I'm worried about. I mean, what the *hell* are *you* going to *do* in *Baton Rouge, Louisiana?*

A good question indeed. But the point isn't that my neighbor had managed to quadruple my anxiety on this subject; nor was it that she frequently spoke in italics; the point, rather, was that she cared at all. Because what had happened in Washington was that—while I was busy changing diapers and warding off panic attacks—I'd actually found myself a home. My butter compartment was filled with borrowed sticks of butter, my twins were wearing clothes that had once belonged to the family four houses down, and Sam didn't appear to take after either myself or my husband, but after Jeremy, the kid who lived across the street.

The For Sale sign sat like a giant taunt on our front lawn, and every few days some recently married lawyer-lawyer couple would spend about two seconds deciding that our house—that I'd spent the morning cleaning—was too small, until finally, after months of agony, we managed to sell it at a loss. Then Jeremy's mother called from across the street to invite us to a farewell party.

The thing I liked about this party was: It was a potluck vegetarian party, and since we were the guests of honor, we didn't have to bring so much as a cherry tomato. The other thing I liked about it was: My husband and I wouldn't get lost trying to find our way there, and then spend the next hour driving around in circles and not stopping at a gas station to get directions—on the theory that my husband can "sense" that we're "getting there"—and finally get into a fight about whose fault it was that we missed the exit.

All our neighbors came—Janet and Andy, Jim and Colleen, Polly and Don, Janyne and Bill—and they all sat around the back yard, looking at us like we had lost our minds and had actually decided to give up our lives in a place where there are tons of great restaurants and fabulous museums and so many smart overly educated competitive types that you can't walk out the door without bumping into a former Rhodes scholar, to move to a state where they eat alligator.

The other thing the guests were doing—I mean, other than gaze at us in an effort to determine whether we were suffering some odd form of joint dementia—was eating. It was a fabulous spread—hummus and pasta salads and a big bowl of marinated grilled vegetables that were as good as any I've tasted. It was the earthy, messy food that I happen to love, the kind, indeed, that is impossible not to spill, and hence complemented not only my own personal fashion style, but also that of all the other guests at our farewell party. Because the thing about Washingtonians is: They may all have graduated from Harvard Law School, but none of them can dress worth a damn. It is the capital city of *shlepp,* a place where wearing a blue, rather than a gray, suit to work passes for high style, and what the men wear is even worse.

So it didn't faze me at all when various pieces of my dinner landed on my front, especially the mixed grilled vegetables, which were so pretty that they improved my appearance. Here's the recipe:

Ingredients: balsamic vinegar, olive oil, lemon, portobello mushrooms, red onions, multicolored bell peppers.

Borrow charcoal from your neighbor, and light the barbecue. Combine vinegar and olive oil (in a ratio of two to one, respectively), lemon juice, and grated lemon rind in a bowl. Slice up the veggies. Brush with liquid. Grill. Serve at room temperature, with beer, on a warm afternoon. Warm? Washington warm? Not compared to where you're headed, sister.

I knew I would miss my neighbors, the people who had populated my daily life, making it rich and sweet, and even I couldn't believe we were leaving them.

But *hey,* like all the women in my family, I'm a trouper. Not only was I ready to completely uproot myself and my three little kids and move fifteen hundred miles away from the nearest psychoanalytically trained psychotherapist, but I wasn't even a little bit scared about whether anyone would want to talk to me once they actually met me. I had the perfect southern belle resumé, after all: Not only am I not precisely fashionable, but also I'm given to fits of hysteria over nothing; in addition none of my ancestors owned slaves, although some of them—going way back—no doubt *were* slaves; I've never met a tennis ball I could hit; I loathe football; I think golf is stupid; I don't like to drive; I'm prone to anxiety attacks in shopping malls. But if my husband was happy, then I was too. After all, I thought, at least one of us will get to have a career, and, like countless "supportive" wives before me, I always had the option of curling up and dying a spiritual, emotional, and intellectual death while my husband went out and made a name for his stupid old selfish self. We were moving to the Deep South, as far south as you can go before you plop into the Gulf of Mexico. Why should I be worried just because the only Jew most people in Baton Rouge had laid eyes on was Jerry Seinfeld, only they didn't get his sense of humor?

We moved in July, which is not a good time of year in Louisiana. (The good time of year is: January third through January sixth.) The problem with July in Louisiana is that it's a tad warm. Warm as a sauna. Warm as a steam bath. Warm as a boiler room. Okay, so most people don't bother to come outside until December—that's why God created air-conditioning. Plus there are the daily afternoon hurricanes, when the sky turns green and the trees shake back and forth and all the lizards that are supposed to live outside come inside, change into their loungewear, and watch *Oprah*.

Actually, the move wasn't as awful as I'd anticipated. It wasn't as awful as I'd anticipated in part because Grandma Lola, who *is* a trouper, came to help. She kept looking around our new house and saying, "Why does everything smell like bacon grease? Oi, the goyim, haven't they ever heard that you are what you cook?" The other reason it wasn't as awful as I'd anticipated was that, within minutes of our arrival, people we'd never before so much as *heard* of started calling us on the phone to invite us over to dinner.

It just didn't seem possible that so many people were so . . . *friendly.* Didn't they know that the proper way to treat strangers was with snide superiority? Didn't they know that the first thing you're supposed to say when you meet someone new is: "I went to Harvard Law School. Where did you go?" Followed by: "My practice chiefly involves arguing before the Supreme Court. What do *you* do?" But the friendliness was the real thing, and bit by bit our new neighbors dropped by "with a little old something I whipped up, nothing much," in the form of cakes and pies, and within about a week, just about every Jew in town knew of our arrival, and had invited us over for a typical *Shabbos* dinner of, say, shrimp étouffée.

One of the yummiest treats that arrived on our doorstep was a cake that one of our new neighbors,

Carol Anne, had made for us, from scratch, and then set on a plate covered with leaves and flowers from her garden. "Just a little ole somethin' for y'all," she said, by way of explanation. Later she told me that the recipe was a well-known one in this part of the world. By this time, I'd gained approximately fifty pounds, on cakes and pies alone. Here is the recipe:

2 cups sugar

1½ cups butter

1½ cups oil

5 eggs, separated

1 teaspoon baking soda

1 cup buttermilk

2 cups flour

1 cup canned, flaked coconut

½ teaspoon butter flavoring

½ teaspoon vanilla

Cream sugar, butter, and oil; add egg yolks, While beating, stir soda into buttermilk; add butter mixture and flour to batter. Fold in coconut. Beat egg whites and fold into mixture. Add flavorings. Pour batter into three greased, floured nine-inch pans. Bake at 350 degrees for twenty-five minutes. Cool and frost.

Frosting
8 ounces cream cheese

½ cup butter

1 pound confectionery sugar

1½ cups chopped pecans

½ teaspoon butter flavoring

½ teaspoon vanilla

Combine cream cheese and butter; beat in sugar; add pecans and flavorings.

One late afternoon when the temperatures had plummeted into the low nineties and, having devoured Carol Anne's cake, I was seriously considering emergency liposuction, I took a walk with my kids. We'd just turned the corner into the next street when a woman I'd never before laid eyes on came up to me, introduced herself, and invited me and the children to her house for lunch the following week. She said that she wanted to introduce me to another young mom who had recently moved into the neighborhood, which was an extremely flattering way to phrase her invitation, given that I was kind of inching up toward forty. Needless to say, I didn't correct her.

On the appointed day, the twins and I dressed in our best everyday *shlepp*-wear—me in this cute little denim jumper that I'd bought from a catalogue before I knew what pregnancy was going to do to my legs, and the twins in delightful matching outfits of stained T-shirts and slightly misshapen shorts—and walked the two blocks to our neighbor's house. (Sam's new school had started up by then.) I was carrying a diaper bag filled with *shmutz*. And the twins were carrying their own equipment—in the case of Jonathan: two cardboard toilet paper rolls, an orange plastic hammer, and a large, interesting stick he'd found in our back yard; in the case of Rose: a used-up lipstick, a pair of blue plastic pliers, and a copy of the Triple-A Road Service manual that Grandma Lola had left behind.

When we got to the house, I happened to notice that we were not the only guests. Indeed, the living room was filled with a dozen or so young, well-groomed blonde women wearing clean pastel silk and linen suits, holding their clean infants, also attired in clean pastel suits. I immediately discerned that the twins and I may have made a mistake in the fashion department. But it was too late. We'd been spotted, by our hostess of all people, who took me by the hand, led me into the living room, and began to introduce me around.

The problem was this: I should never have accepted the luncheon invitation to begin with. In fact, the very idea of going out to lunch makes me quake with anxiety. I always feel overexposed in the bright white light of the day. I spill my lightly sautéed trout almondine on my blouse, and talk too much. And this was worse; this was much *much* worse: This was a ladies' lunch, and all the ladies, with the exception of me, were—as it turned out—talking about chintz. Chintz for the window treatment. Chintz for the sofa. Chintz for the throw pillows. I stood there with a stupid, fake smile on my face, knowing that at any instant now one of the blonde moms was going to turn to me and ask me whether I always suffered from having such an excess of saliva in my mouth.

Lunch was served. In the dining room. On *china*. Even in my panic, I understood that our hostess had truly put on the dog. She'd made a delicious chicken salad and served it with—what else?—iced tea. She'd even made mini-peanut-butter-and-jelly sandwiches for the children.

I'm not even a tiny bit shy, yet as I sat there, trying my best not to eat too fast or splatter mayonnaise down my front, I felt as if I were once again in the seventh grade, where I'd spend a dozen or so years as the ultimate self-chosen outcast. Was all of Baton Rouge like this? The last time I'd attended anything similar had been almost a decade earlier, at my own bridal shower, at my sister's Upper West Side apartment, and there the talk had revolved mainly around psychoanalysis—my own as well as those of my girlfriends. So all the talk about chintz, which eventually evolved into a conversation about the sororities the other moms had pledged when they'd been undergraduates at LSU, kind of left me in a conversational end zone.

Jonathan found me at the dining room table, climbed onto my lap, and brought his orange plastic hammer down on my plate of chicken salad, splattering the contents all over our hostess's Oriental rug, and hitting one of the blonde moms in the eye. She wiped it away with a corner of her linen napkin and looked at me as if she were thinking of mounting a pogrom.

"I have big poop," Jonathan said.

It was all a little embarrassing, but somehow or another I got through it without saying anything really stupid or embarrassing such as: What the FUCK am I doing here in the middle of *Gidget Meets Gone with the Fucking Wind?* And the kids did all right, too, once they discovered how much fun it was to throw pieces of their peanut-butter-and-jelly sandwiches into the backyard goldfish pond.

When my husband got home from his new, professorial job that he totally loved, I calmly explained to him why I was taking the children and moving back to someplace civilized, such as New York. No matter that my new house was about twenty times bigger than my old one; no matter that both of the two rabbis in town had stopped off at our house to say "Shalom y'all"; no matter that, once I moved, I'd probably never have sex again, or at least not with my husband. "Fuck fuck fuck fuck fuck," is what, more or less, comprised the gist of my argument.

"Hey," said Sam, running into the room. "*Fuck* and *suck* rhyme."

"Good going, Jen," my husband said.

"I'm going to write a poem about it," Sam continued.

I just knew that I'd never have friends again, and

that I'd be isolated in my weird egotistic self-pitying narcissistic struggle with myself for the rest of
my life, and I'd end up one of those wretched
embittered old women whose own grandchildren don't
want to kiss them because they smell bad. Baton Rouge
seemed like a very bad idea.

Except maybe it wasn't. My husband, who tends to
be rational and fair, pointed out the obvious: that
someone I didn't know had bothered to welcome me
into her home and introduce me to people she thought
I'd like to meet. He also said, in his calm, annoying
way, that no one had so much as hinted that they
would like to burn a cross in our front yard, nor had
anyone we'd met since our arrival been anything other
than warm and welcoming—the parade of cakes and
pies in fact had not yet ended. Finally he said that, unlike in Washington, we might actually meet some people in Baton Rouge who weren't lawyers.

A week or so after the ladies' lunch, one of the
young blonde moms—Catherine, the original young
blonde mom I was supposed to meet—dropped by
with her little daughter. We sat outside in the garden. It
was different this time. We talked about all kinds of
things, but there was no mention of chintz. As time
went on, Catherine and I became friends, just like we
were supposed to.

Salad Days

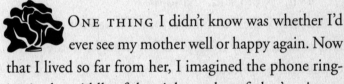 ONE THING I didn't know was whether I'd ever see my mother well or happy again. Now that I lived so far from her, I imagined the phone ringing in the middle of the night, and my father's voice on the end of the line, saying, "Get on the next plane," which is problematic under any circumstances, given that, as far as I can tell, most airplanes are held together with Band-aids. I imagined that the next time we were together, it would be at her bedside. I imagined telling Sam—who adored her—that Grammy wouldn't be with us much longer. I imagined how betrayed he'd feel.

But in early November, my father called not to announce that Mom had made her reservation for her trip to the Hereafter, but that the two of them were coming to Baton Rouge for a visit, which for some people is kind of the same thing, but that's the subject of my next book.

It was Mom's first trip since she'd been diagnosed with cancer, and I didn't know what to expect. But at half-past one, Mom and Dad pulled into my driveway in a rented car. The kids ran out to greet them, and Mom popped her head, now covered with soft gray curls, out.

"This isn't so terrible," she said, looking up and down the street.

"What did you expect?" I said. "That rednecks in pickup trucks would drive by every few minutes to spray a swastika on our front door?"

"Well," Mom said. "Kind of."

But my father, who never much cared for chit-chat, and never had any trouble getting straight to the point, changed the subject.

"We haven't had lunch," he said. "What have you got?"

So I made a pasta salad, heated up a loaf of bread, and served lunch outside, in the garden.

Here's the recipe I used:

Any kind of smallish pasta, like medium shells, or
     corkscrews, or bows
Any kind of smallish cut-up vegetable-like things, like
     olives, artichoke hearts, red bell pepper, carrots, snap
     peas, broccoli, etc.

1 can tuna fish, drained
1 cup olive oil
½ cup balsamic vinegar
2 tablespoons mayonnaise
1 tablespoon Dijon mustard
1 teaspoon sugar

Cook the pasta the usual way. Meanwhile, chop up all the vegetable-like things. Drain pasta; run cold water over it to cool. Combine with vegetables and tuna fish. In a mixing bowl, combine oil, vinegar, mayo, mustard, and sugar. Pour over salad. Toss. Serve on pretty plates, in your beautiful lush garden with its exotic lilies and crazily flowering vines and apricot-scented air, because this is Louisiana, where the sun shines in November, and the deep brilliant blueness of the sky is a miracle to behold.

"It's so beautiful here," Mom told me, looking around the garden. "Enjoy it, honey. Enjoy your life. You've got to stop eating your own liver out. Life's too short." Then Dad said that maybe Baton Rouge wasn't so bad for a cow town, and would I like to see the op-ed piece he was working on for the *Washington Post*? As he got up to help himself to seconds, Mom said, "He may not be perfect, but at least he takes the garbage out."

That night, Grandma Lola called to find out what the children might like for Hanukkah, which was coming up in less than seven weeks and had I yet had a

chance to meet the local literary lights such as
Anne Rice and Andrei Codrescu so that I could
invite them to dinner, after which they'd be sure
to introduce me to their publishers? I told her that
Mom and Dad were visiting, and that Mom, despite all
those months of injesting poison, was amazingly re-
silient. I told her that Mom had told me to stop worrying. Grandma Lola said: "Your mother's absolutely
right. You can't go around getting an ulcer all the time.
Darling, don't you know that these are your lettuce
days?"

Then she asked to speak to Mom, and for about an
hour, the two of them, who had, over the years, become
each other's advocates in their ongoing war against the
parents of their grandchildren, cracked jokes at my ex-
pense.

"Are you on Prozac finally?" Mom said when she got
off the phone. "You don't seem quite as incredibly tense
as you used to."

It was true. Though I was far from home—though I
was now a wandering Jew in the Bible belt—I grew
steadily more light-hearted.

At Hanukkah, my neighbors came over to say,
"Happy Hanukkah, y'all." At Passover, they said: "*Lais-
sez les bons temps rouler.*"

They say that alligator tastes like chicken and that
nutria is delicious. Football is worshipped. Outside
there are snakes and fire ants, and lizards that crawl
through the crack under my front door and shimmy up

the stairs to my bedroom to say "Howdy, folks!" while I'm sleeping. Jesus is alive in everyday matters, and the earth is filled with the spirits of the fallen and the damned.

I had landed in a world of *boudin* and bayous, humidity and hurricanes, petty politics, blatant corruption, the delta blues, Dixieland, racism, and magnificent generosity of the spirit. The day I sat with my parents in my beautiful garden, it began to dawn on me that simple happiness had been given to me—for I'd been lucky, always. My mother was alive, my father was by her side, my husband was happy, my children were healthy, and I had entered my salad days.